JOHN CALVIN Versus THE WESTMINSTER CONFESSION

JOHN CALVIN

VERSUS

THE WESTMINSTER CONFESSION

Holmes Rolston, III

JOHN KNOX PRESS
Richmond, Virginia

Library of Congress Cataloging in Publication Data

Rolston, Holmes, 1932-
    John Calvin versus the Westminster Confession.

    Includes bibliographical references.
    1. Westminster Assembly of Divines. The Confession of faith. 2. Calvin,
Jean, 1509-1564—Theology.
I.   Title.
BX9183.R63   230.4′2′0924   75-37422
ISBN 0-8042-0488-8

© John Knox Press 1972

Printed in the United States of America

Preface

I do not write dispassionately, yet I hope objectively to approximate the truth in a critical chapter of Reformed history. But this backward look is with the present in mind. We have entered a generation of stirring; there is hardly a Presbyterian denomination which has not faced confessional revision. There is much resistance; only one such body has succeeded in revising in the twentieth century what was fixed in the seventeenth. The Reformed church must again be ever reforming—*ecclesia reformata sed semper reformanda*. From here onward, it will take increasingly difficult discernment to maintain a Reformed witness. This work is a contribution to that task. It is, in short, a radical questioning of the Westminster Confession of Faith in defense of the Reformed faith.

I may be pardoned, I hope, if I am now and again polemical. Those assumptions of the Westminster Confession against which I inveigh with most heat are presuppositions of which I myself was too long a victim. This study is a kind of veiled autobiography, a report of the healing of some spiritual disorders. I found myself oppressed by a theological establishment, and there are no moments in my life closer to moments of conversion than those flashes of insight after hours of pain in which I was given to escape and to overthrow, alas, the treasured confession of my mother church. Every man who thinks far enough finds himself oppressed with dualisms and bifurcations of one kind or another: mind and matter, freedom and determinism, causality and teleology, noumena and phenomena, appearance and reality, monisms and pluralisms, immanence and transcendence, the sacred and the secular, nature and grace; and if ever one rids himself of them, it is a relief. The dualism that afflicted me most grievously was that between law and gospel, justice and grace, works and faith, and I was greatly redeemed when I cast out this incubus.

5

But I came to find in my struggle for spiritual health that the disease which afflicted me was a plague that had long infected the Reformed churches. And to my dismay, one of the principal reservoirs of infection was at once the wellspring of faith, the Westminster Confession. True enough that many others had developed immunity to this systemic pollution, but now I detected that the poison sapped more strength than was noticed. And it could, as it had done with me, work much mischief. So I resolved to clear from my community the disorder from which I had been cured, and hence this work. If I am right, few things can rival the importance for Reformed theology of having thought its way clear of the undesirable legacies of the most classic of its creeds.

The medicine that broke the fever I was to find in the Reformer himself. It was Calvin who rescued me from the Calvinists. I at first found this odd, for there was much in him that I had had to revise. I had never, for all my rearing, been particularly attracted to the father of my church, and I was, and remain, somewhat apologetic about being a Calvinist. But as I ponder this now, I think it not so strange. The life of the Christian community has more often than not seen the periodic rediscovery of the primacy of grace, achieved by breaking free from an oppressive and frequently legalistic religious establishment. Witness the ministries of Jesus or of Paul against the then prevailing rigidities of Judaism, or the spiritual struggles of Augustine, or Luther's agony in shaking himself free from medieval Catholicism, or Wesley's heart strangely warmed after the moralistic chill of deism, or Barth's joyous "Nein" to the anthropocentric focus of liberal theology. Like Luther, and for all the faults and inadequacies of both Reformers, Calvin was essentially a freedom fighter who had seen the primacy of the grace of God. But disciples are never quite up to the insights of their masters, and the legalisms from which Calvin had escaped had in the century following settled back in across his church. There lies at the head of most, perhaps all, great religious movements a profound capturing or recapturing of deep and nourishing religious insights, and it was not surprising that I had found such vitality at the source of my own heritage. How profound the insight that the church is never so reformed as not to be *semper reformanda!*

The *Ioannis Calvini Opera* in the *Corpus Reformatorum* (abbreviated C.R.), edited by G. Baum, E. Cunitz, and E. Reuss (Brunswick, 1869–1896), has been my normative Reformation text in Latin and in French. Calvin has been translated well and poorly and anciently and not at all. Translations here from Calvin's better known works follow for the most part the standard translations, e.g., the Allen edition of the *Institutes* and the Calvin Translation Society series of the commentaries. But I adapt these to the definitive *Corpus Reformatorum* text. Translations of the sermons are my own. The text of the Westminster Confession is that in present use in the Presbyterian Church, U.S., which where we consult it is unaltered from the 1646 original. Despite the fact that federal theology is the official position of the Presbyterian churches, other original federal writings are for the most part available only in compends or in antiquated editions, often untranslated. I sometimes adapt existing translations, but more often make my own. A synopsis of this study appeared in the *Scottish Journal of Theology,* Vol. 23, No. 2 (May 1970), pp. 129–156; I must also record with thanks much assistance given me by Dr. T. F. Torrance of the University of Edinburgh.

Contents

1. The Westminster Confession and Covenant Theology   11
2. Calvin and the Order of Grace   23
3. Man: His Duty and His Sin   38
4. Law in Covenant and Nature   58
5. The Righteousness of God   72
6. Responsible Man: His Accountability   86
7. Irresponsible Man: His Culpability   99
8. Reformed Responsible Man   111
Notes   117

CHAPTER 1

The Westminster Confession
and Covenant Theology

The Confession of 1967 in the United Presbyterian Church marks officially the beginning of the end of the four-century Presbyterian venture into covenant theology. Southern cousins in the Presbyterian Church, U.S., are now facing similar retirement of their historic confession. Perhaps they will, perhaps not. The Westminster Confession remains the prime confessional document of many Presbyterians, as for instance in the Scots and British parent churches, and in many smaller Presbyterian bodies. Even in the United Church, the Westminster Confession remains in the showroom of creeds.

But we have recently seen one breach in the federal principle so long enshrined in the Westminster standards, and others will follow, increasingly to mark the scheme where it yet remains creedal formula as a theological anachronism no longer to be regarded seriously but to be suffered as historical background. With the hold of federal theology officially beginning to break, we can turn to survey that curious but historic route. Seen from its concept of a responsible man, we here argue, that route has been a prolonged detour away from the insights of the Reformers. We shall challenge afresh the assumption that the Calvinism of the Westminster Confession is true to the Reformer himself. Indeed, it has seldom been realized by persons otherwise well versed in the Reformed tradition that the twin covenant tectonics which dominates the substructure of all later Reformed dogmatics is totally absent from Calvin. Worse than that, its fundamental incompatibility with Calvin's thought has gone all but unnoticed.

1. Covenant Theology: Its Rise to Dominance

In two generations after the death of Calvin there appeared

several variations of a theological format involving dual covenants, a model which matured in the contrasting *covenant of works* and *covenant of grace* of the Westminster Confession. So marked a characteristic did this become that the central stream of the Reformed faith took its name from the Latin word for covenant, *foedus,* the federal or covenant theology. The precise historical origin of the conjugate covenants is an interesting and as yet somewhat incompleted study in the now relatively obscure theologians who followed Calvin. We here can but outline its post-Reformation origin.

The notion seems to have entered with the *Loci Communes* (1560) of Wolfgang Musculus (1497-1563), who in contrast with his fellow Reformers, divides the one covenant into two, a "general covenant" of God with the universe and a "special covenant" of God with the elect.[1] A little afterward, the division of a "covenant of nature" and a "covenant of grace" was introduced by Zacharias Ursinus (1534-1583), an author of the powerful Heidelberg Catechism. *Foederaltheologie* was taught in systematic form in the Dutch universities of the seventeenth century by a notable sequence: Johann Koch, or (in Latin) Cocceius (1603-1669); his pupil Francis Burmann (1628-1679); and Burmann's successor, Herman Witsius (1636-1708).[2] Covenant theology was established in the Swiss church even earlier than in the Dutch, and later taught just as ably. Amandus Polanus (1561-1610) preceded Cocceius; J. H. Heidegger (1633-1698) was his contemporary and friend. Then federal theology reached its full flower in Calvin's own Genevan church in the teaching of Francis Turretin (1623-1687), author of the long-standard Reformed text known as Turretin's *Institutes.*[3]

Covenant theology was once assumed to be continental in origin, and doubtless it has continental ancestry. But there is also evidence that as a true theological system it was born and reared on Scots and English soil. Robert Rollock (1555-1599), first principal of the University of Edinburgh, wrote of "God's two covenants, both that of works and that of grace," and in his *Treatise on Effectual Calling* (1597) is found the important term "covenant of works," a term which earlier had seen little or no use.[4] Also early and little noticed is the work of Dudley Fenner (1558?-1587), a young English associate of Thomas Cartwright, who while exiled in Holland published his *Sacra Theologia* (1585), utilizing a carefully worked out covenant of works set opposite a covenant of grace.[5]

Whatever its precise origin, within a few decades the covenant scheme became something received as though it were apostolic. It was a characteristic of English Puritanism, seen, for instance, in Edward Fisher's *Marrow of Modern Divinity* (1645) or in William Ames, and in a variant form in John Ball.[6] The scheme was given full confessional status for the first time in the Westminster Confession of Faith in 1646, although it had earlier appeared in the Irish Articles, and in this form it thereafter prevailed in Reformed thought. Rooted so firmly in the confessional standards of the church, the scheme was repeated and elaborated by virtually all subsequent theologians who considered themselves disciples of Calvin. From these Old World sources it appeared in American Presbyterianism, taught at Princeton for more than half a century by the nineteenth century's most esteemed American theologian, Charles Hodge (1797–1878).[7] It was one of the prime requisites of sound orthodoxy. Where it was recognized that the concept was not in Calvin, this was considered a positive development of his thought, even with occasional criticism of Calvin for not having adequately formulated the concept.[8]

Despite the fact that the first framers of covenant theology were soon forgotten men—partly because but few of their writings survived the transition from Latin to English, partly because Hodge and others who repeated substantially what they had said were nearer at hand—the system they founded long retained not merely wide prevalence in but control of the Presbyterian churches. Through its confessional status and presence in the catechisms, it remained the official theology of all major Presbyterian bodies of both Britain and America until the recent adoption of the Confession of 1967. Even in churches adhering to the great mid-sixteenth-century Reformed confessions formed before the advent of covenant theology (Heidelberg Catechism, Belgic Confession, Second Helvetic Confession), it is the orthodox theology. By way of English Puritanism, it is widely dispersed in Baptist churches, and is not without considerable influence generally in the Protestant tradition.

In the twentieth century, despite its official presence in the confessional standards, and despite advocates such as Benjamin Warfield, W. G. T. Shedd, and Louis Berkhof, Reformed theology as characteristically preached came to give less and less formal allegiance to the doctrine of the covenants. But the reason was never primarily a dissatisfaction with the scheme as such. It broke up in the turbulence of theological thinking in this century when concepts of the origin of man so radically altered that the idea of a divine covenant with all men in Adam no longer had force. The doctrine of the covenants is now bypassed as a mythological and innocuous relic not really affecting the Confession's system of doctrine. But that the doctrine of the covenants was discredited from without and never really from within the church has not been an altogether unmixed blessing. It has meant that the formal expression of a covenant of works was abandoned, often to leave the church unaware of a legacy of implications yet seeping through the understanding of God, man, sin, and responsibility. When the broadening authority of science forbade the chronology and historicity of a first covenant, it did not touch the central motif of that covenant: law. Here Reformed thought had neither need nor desire to recant. On the contrary, the notion of law was amenable to scientific and philosophical thought.

These covenants were long taken literally, even though the more sophisticated writers knew that there was in them much symbolism representing and conveying spiritual truths. But they can be taken seriously even after they are no longer taken literally. When the myth of the covenants was exploded, the facts were nowhere denied; they were simply reallocated. Behind the myth was this reality: the primacy of law. So Reformed theology replaced the default of a primal, historical covenant, initially by Adam and subsequently by all, with the continuing, perennial default of a moral law, innate and internal in all. Sired by the mythological original, this symbol system proved eminently adaptable to the modern temper, or, perhaps more accurately, to certain moods in it. So there has remained a sort of anonymous presence of the doctrine of the covenants which matches its official presence, even where the confessional presence was admitted to be anachronistic. Reformed theologians wrote uninhibitedly, and altogether without embarrassment, of the primacy of law. Thus the broken symbol functioned still, and has had a longer reach across Reformed theology than is generally supposed.

2. The Covenant of Works

God made with Adam—so orthodoxy maintained—a covenant of works, and in Adam the covenant was made with all mankind. The Westminster Confession is terse and precise:

> The first covenant made with man was a covenant of works, wherein life was promised to Adam, and in him to his posterity, upon condition of perfect and personal obedience.[9]

Because of this brevity we must elaborate by listening to commentators and other defenders of the doctrine—a procedure we shall often be using to make explicit what is confessionally implicit. The *Institutes* of Turretin contains the mature system and gives us a fuller hearing.

> This double covenant is proposed to us in Scripture: of nature and of grace, of works and of faith, legal and evangelical. The foundation of this distinction rests both on different characteristics in God as he contracts, who can be considered now as Creator and Lord, then as Redeemer and Father, and on the diverse condition of man, who may be viewed either as perfect or as a fallen creature; and on the diverse mode of obtaining life and happiness, either by one's own obedience, or by another's obedience imputed to us, and on the diverse duties prescribed to man, to wit, works or faith.
>
> For in the former, God as Creator demands perfect obedience from innocent man with the promise of eternal happiness and life; but in the latter, God as Father promises salvation in Christ to the fallen man, under the condition of faith. The former rests upon the work of man, the latter upon the grace of God alone; the former upon a just Creator, the latter upon a merciful Redeemer; the former was made with innocent man without a Mediator; the latter with fallen man, by the intervention of a Mediator.[10]

After more than a century of service, this Latin text of the last great orthodox teacher of the Genevan church passed out of use, and the English *Systematic Theology* of Hodge carried this teaching forward, unchanged, through the nineteenth century and into the twentieth.

This covenant is based on divine *law* and *justice;* it is a *legal,* in contrast to an *evangelical,* covenant. The idea for this covenant was educed from the Mosaic law, where in covenant (at least it was argued) God promised life on condition of obedience; this covenant idea, removed from its Old Testament setting, has been pushed back to creation and made the basic relationship between God and man. An idea which does in a limited way belong to God's dealing with Israel becomes the original divine order instituted at creation. Covenant theologians discuss at some length the relationship between the Mosaic covenant and the covenant of works. There is a mixing at Sinai with the Abrahamic covenant of grace, but the Mosaic covenant per se has its closest affinity with the covenant of creation. The federalists find some differences, but the two are closely connected, at times virtually identical, apart from the ceremonial law and even though the covenant of grace was in effect prior to this giving of the law. Scriptural support for the covenant of works—indeed the covenant vocabulary itself, as this could not be found in Genesis 1—2 or elsewhere in unambiguous reference to creation—is freely taken from the Mosaic code. Turretin, Witsius, and others, for instance, cite Leviticus 18:5, "If a man do these statutes, he shall live in them."[11]

This is a covenant of *works,* the emphasis on merit being all the greater when set in opposition to the later covenant of grace. The "condition" of the covenant, man's duty, according to Turretin, is *not faith, but works.* It is therefore premised on such things as man's virtue, strength, credit, worth, and ability, and the proposed "reward" is a kind of payment. The language is highly contractual, which accords well with its legalism. In this covenant every man gets his due. It supposes a proper or an "inherent righteousness" as distinct from an "imputed righteousness."[12]

The covenant of works, it is true, is set within the framework of a "condescension on God's part" (Westminster Confession).[13] Reformed thought usually and often carefully recognized that Adam needed and received some "aid of grace."[14] Adam "had not sufficient strength not to be in need of God's further grace and help in order not to sin."[15] Nor were these works exclusively thought of as works of merit. Rollock could call them "pledges of thankfulness,"[16] a delightful expression. But most writers make the distinction this way: No merit of man can be "intrinsic"; all must be on the basis of covenant, *ex pacto,* yet within the covenant, merit may be "inherent" in man. Calvin had spoken of the merit of works *ex pacto* in connection with the Mosaic covenant, and this is transferred to the universal covenant of works made with all mankind. But federal thought could not really take these reservations seriously. That it is by name a covenant of works has a very deadening effect on anything said about grace. The overall emphasis was that God did not come to primal man in a relationship of grace, for man did not yet need that grace, but stood by his works. All too typical is the teaching in a Scots Bible class handbook:

> By the creature's own natural strength is the covenant to be fulfilled. Grace may have been shown in the condescension that entered into a covenant, but the covenant in its terms is not of grace but of works.[17]

This is a covenant of *nature,* a term which becomes (despite variations in Ursinus and other pre-federal writers) but an alternate name for the covenant of works. Again, the term is guarded so that the natural relationship is not intrinsic. The nature with which God endowed man at creation is described in this covenant.

> The covenant of nature is that which God, the Creator, made with innocent man as his creature, concerning the giving to him of eternal happiness and life under the condition of perfect and personal obedience. It is called natural, not from natural obligation, which God has not toward man; but because it is founded on the nature of man, as it was first created by God, and on man's integrity or powers.[18]

The term is apt, moreover, because of the connection with the law of nature written on man's heart, so that man naturally and apart from revelation knows this covenant. The exact relationship between the covenant of works and the law of nature was variously conceived, but there was always a partial equation of the two.

> It may also be recognized naturally that there is a covenant intervening between God and man. Man's conscience keeps asserting that to God the Creator and Lord of man obedience on his part

> as a creature is bound to be enjoined. . . . Man is not naturally
> ignorant of the promise of God in promising good to the obe-
> dient.[19]

Of the various terms employed, covenant of *life* is the most
promising, and unfortunately the least employed. It might have
been used to lessen the strong emphasis on man's works and to
redress the balance with the covenanting grace of God. The condition of obedience would not have been a meritorious consideration but perhaps a "pledge of thankfulness," simply the *sine qua
non* without which the gift could not be conferred. But it is indica-
tive of the mood of covenant theology that the term was not extensively employed. The Westminster Confession does not use it,
though interestingly the Catechisms show a certain preference for
it. Many leading exponents do not use it at all, or if so only to
identify it with the covenant of works. It becomes a synonymous
term, used merely to indicate that *life* was the reward involved. It
is "called a covenant of life, because life was promised as the reward
of obedience" (Hodge).[20]

Man—mankind in Adam—soon broke in sin the covenant of
works. But is the covenant also broken by God, after it is broken
by man? The federal thinkers explore this question at length.
Cocceius described everything to follow as a series of progressively
greater abrogations of the first covenant, but orthodoxy did not
follow him. The consensus is rather that, though we speak of a
certain antiquation of it for believers, there are most important
ways in which neither sin nor the coming of the covenant of
grace abrogates the legal covenant. The Westminster standards
specify repeatedly that the first covenant was perpetual, and, moreover, this accounts for man's continuing fallen estate. This passage
from the Confession is from the chapter on the law of God:

> God gave to Adam a law, as a covenant of works, by which he
> bound him and all his posterity to personal, entire, exact, and
> perpetual obedience; promised life upon the fulfilling, and threat-
> ened death upon the breach of it; and endued him with power
> and ability to keep it. This law, after his fall, continued to be a
> perfect rule of righteousness . . .

It continues with the claim that "the moral law doth forever bind
all," exempting none from its performance, "although true be-

lievers be not under the law as a covenant of works."[21] All others remain under the force of the general covenant, and from this derives their duty, sin, and judgment.

Witsius entitles a chapter in his *Economy of the Covenants:* "Of the Abrogation of the Covenant of Works on the Part of God." But he devotes most of the chapter to ways that the covenant is "on no account abolished."

> This for us is certain, that many things in this covenant are of immovable and eternal truth, which we recite in this order: (1) The precepts of the covenant . . . bind one and all to a perfect performance of duty, in whatever state they are. (2) The eternal life promised by the covenant cannot be obtained on any other condition than that of perfect obedience in every detail. (3) No disobedience escapes God's vengeance, and death is always the punishment of sin.[22]

The eternal life promised therein can no longer be attained by way of conditional meritorious obedience; not that God has canceled the offer, but that man has incapacitated himself, and hence the covenant is of no help to man. But it is still very much in force. With one or two peripheral exceptions, all covenant writers insist on this.

> Still the covenant of works ought not to be regarded as so abrogated, as though no part of it had place today in the sinner. It is abrogated only as a benefit which can no longer justify or sanctify or glorify man, but it has not been abrogated as a duty and an obligation. Man should be bound to perfect observation of the natural law in this covenant to eternity.[23]

Hodge has a section in his *Systematic Theology* entitled "Perpetuity of the Covenant of Works." It so remains that if man could fulfill the covenant of works he could now be saved in this way.

This conception of the covenant of works as unbroken from the side of God, even when man defaults, is the basis of the eternal principles of justice, instituted by God, which he still holds in force. God still deals with mankind in general on the basis of this first covenant. He binds all to the performance of this covenant; duty and responsibility are so determined, and for this man is held accountable. Even after the superposition of the covenant of grace and for those embraced by the new covenant, the old covenant has force. Though adopted into the evangelical covenant, man is "born under"[24] the legal covenant. Until he is born again, and in some respects even after his regeneration, his nature is so determined and his need of salvation uncovered by it.

3. The Covenant of Grace

There is a second act to this great cosmic drama. Over against the general covenant of works, there is established the special covenant of grace, where God freely gives what he had before promised in reward for the condition of perfect obedience. Here is the Confession's account:

> Man, by his fall, having made himself incapable of life by that covenant [of works], the Lord was pleased to make a second, commonly called the covenant of grace: wherein he freely offered unto sinners life and salvation by Jesus Christ, requiring of them faith in him, that they may be saved, and promising to give unto all those that are ordained unto life, his Holy Spirit, to make them willing and able to believe.[25]

In many writers this covenant is essentially universalistic in theory; they do not hold limited atonement theories. But, though sufficient atonement has been made for all, even these spokesmen are somewhat evasive about whether it is seriously offered to all or to "all who are ordained for life," thus trivializing its universality. Many say that the covenant of grace is made "with believers." It is characteristically narrowed to include only the elect. Be that as it may, the covenant of grace becomes efficacious only for "believers," and nonbelievers derive no benefit or change in status from it. For them it is irrelevant; the *lex generalis* is a *lex talionis*. On this there is consensus. The covenant of grace is God's way of dealing with some men, but not with all men. The rest are dealt with on the basis of the covenant of works.

The only condition on man's part is faith. It is not even a "condition" in the sense in which works were a condition of the first covenant. Many writers will not use the word "condition" here at all, and in the Confession's account of the covenants the linguistic asymmetry is not accidental: the first covenant is made upon "condition" of obedience, but the second "requires" faith. The asymmetry reflects the appearance of grace. God's pure grace is revealed for the first time in this covenant, for it was not really known, or needed, in creation and the previous covenant. God, who was formerly known as Creator, Lord, Lawgiver, condescending though he was earlier, now reveals himself as merciful Father and Redeemer.

The second covenant is made with Adam and his posterity, and administered under different "dispensations" in the time of Adam, Abraham, Moses, and Christ, or under a "twofold economy": in expectation of Christ and in Christ revealed, this latter division being what we normally term the Old and New Testaments. The covenant of grace embraces the whole biblical story and reaches back to paradise. Even when it is sometimes said that this covenant is made with Christ and his heirs, and not with Adam and his heirs as was the first, our first parents are included as heirs of Christ and partakers of the better covenant. "Immediately after the fall God gave to Adam the promise of redemption. . . . This promise was repeated and amplified from time to time, until the Redeemer actually came."[26]

The federalists usually proceeded to greater elaboration of this second covenant. A distinction is drawn between a "covenant of redemption" enacted between God and Christ in eternity, and a "covenant of grace" made between God and man through Christ. The covenanting parties were at times differently stated. But these developments do not occur in the Westminster Confession and are not of importance for our study. The Confession is primarily, of course, given over to an exposition of the grandeur of the covenant of grace, and it receives in its own way much praise there. Soundly biblical when properly developed, this theme became an ancestor of contemporary interest in *Heilsgeschichte*. The intensive and extensive attention Reformed thought gave to the covenant theme was not without many undoubted excellences.

Yet the whole theological enterprise remains colored by the primal covenant. The covenant of grace does not replace the covenant of works, but is worked out and established within it. It is superposed on, it overlies, it interrupts it. "This covenant of grace was not so much set up in room of the covenant of works, as added to it."[27] It is therefore a careless reading of federal theology, though a mistake frequently made, to assume that the covenant of works is no longer important because it has been replaced by the covenant of grace. We cannot dispense with this preface and go on our way freely to develop the main theme of the Confession as though this first covenant had been erased. Rather, it needs to be kept steadily in view. It is the polestar by which we traverse all religious terrain; it fixes the coordinates of our theological geography. The integral man of the first covenant nowhere exists, true enough, but fallen man is born and lives under that covenant. There is hardly a theological category that escapes declension by it. The first covenant remains as the necessary precondition and framework of the second. Chronologically and logically for covenant theology, grace came and comes only after sin. God demonstrates his grace to man only after man is unable to provide his own works. The first covenant overarches and encloses the second. The whole understanding of divine grace has to be worked out as a second covenant introduced with the failure of the first. There is no real cause to speak of the grace of God until after man sins. Grace is a remedy and second resort, however wonderful that remedy may be.

The covenant of grace, moreover, has no real bearing on the essential nature of man. The new covenant does not alter or negate the nature of man's existence, responsibility, or sin. Man may be saved by the grace of God, but he is saved because he could not save himself. Originally and ideally man lives in a relationship to God where he by his own works justifies his existence. This is paradise as it was intended to be. Like the legendary rivers of Eden which flowed out to water the earth, this legal fountain irrigates the whole theological landscape.

CHAPTER 2

Calvin and the Order of Grace

Of all this Calvin knew nothing, for these theological innovations were the work of his successors. Let us now set aside the doctrine of the covenants and examine the teaching of Calvin as it is parallel to and in contrast with the carefully articulated federal system. The task is not an easy one for those long accustomed to reading Calvin with spectacles fashioned by the creedal statements of the following century. But he who comes to inquire of the first-generation Reformer freed from the presuppositions of the Westminster Confession will soon find that there are differences between them of the greatest moment. To be true to Calvin we must not in the beginning speak of the covenant at all, for while he does give prominence later to a single covenant of God with Israel fulfilled in Christ, the polar covenant scheme does not for him form the same kind of underpinning that it soon did for the Calvinists.

The nearest equivalent concept is that of divine *order,* a concept fundamental to Calvin and one which readily integrates the whole of his teaching. The original divine order and its subsequent inversion by sin are concepts in Calvin very nearly parallel to the later notion of a covenant of works and the breaking of that covenant by sin. The will of God is incorporated—"instituted" in the vocabulary of the *Institutes*—into the universe at creation. Let us see this in a little more detail.

1. The Order of Grace

All things are ordered according to the movement of God's grace in creation which is fulfilled in redemption. This includes the universe, the creature, and especially man. Calvin regularly recalls this at critical points of exposition, as for instance "the genu

ine order of nature" introduced early in the opening chapters of
the *Institutes* and repeatedly in his Commentary on Genesis, chapters 1–8. An *order of creation* (*creationis ordo*) gives to the creature
and particularly to man his destiny and reason for being. In this
order man lives in *integrity* (*integritas*) and in *rectitude* (*recti-
tudo*). Men ought to follow "the law of their creation," to live in
the "genuine order."[1]

This is clearly an order of grace, for Calvin speaks simultaneously of both the order and the "divine grace" first instituted.[2]
Man is gifted with life in felicity by his heavenly father. We begin
with what God has done for us. Calvin can be very eloquent about
this. In the Commentary on Genesis, paralleled in the *Institutes,*
Calvin writes:

> In the very order of the creation the paternal solicitude of God
> for man is conspicuous, because he has furnished the world with
> all things needful, and even with an immense profusion of wealth,
> before he formed man. Thus man was rich before he was born.
>
> God himself has demonstrated, by the very order of creation, that
> he made all things for the sake of man. . . . whenever we call
> God the Creator of heaven and earth, let us at the same time
> reflect, that the dispensation of those things which he has made is
> in his own power, and that we are his children, whom he has
> received into his charge and custody, to be supported and educated;
> so that we may expect every blessing from him alone, and cherish
> a certain hope that he will never suffer us to want those things
> which are necessary to our well-being, that our hope may depend
> on no other; that, whatever we need or desire, our prayers may be
> be directed to him, and that, from whatever quarter we receive
> any advantage, we may acknowledge it to be his benefit, and
> confess it with thanksgiving; that, being allured with such great
> sweetness of goodness and beneficence, we may study to love and
> worship him with all our hearts.[3]

Or notice how these themes inform his exegesis when he comes
to a significant passage on man's place in the world, as, for instance, Psalm 8:

> Generally the whole order of this world is arranged and instituted
> so as to promote man's happiness and well-being. . . . But the
> integrity of order which God instituted in the world at the be-
> ginning is now disrupted.[4]

These gifts are of two kinds: natural gifts, such as health and happiness in an ordered society, and supernatural or spiritual gifts, including faith and righteousness which lead to eternal felicity. That the latter are gifts, even for sinless man, will assume significance later in our study. Nor are these gifts static, but rather dynamic. We live not intrinsically, but by "continued inspiration" in a milieu of divine grace. A steady "communication with God was the source of life to Adam."[5]

Grace evokes gratitude. Reciprocal to divine goodness is man's response. While this is for Calvin a complex returning of the whole of man's life to God—a movement that we shall explore when we come to consider the duty of man—it cannot be better or more simply put than to say that man is to answer his God in gratitude. Consider, for instance, how clearly this note sounds in Calvin's remarkable *Instruction in Faith:*

> At first man was formed in the image and resemblance of God in order that man might admire his Author in the adornments with which he had been nobly vested by God and honor him with proper [gratitude].[6]

The Latin *gratitudo* is here an interesting revision in Calvin's own translation of the French of 1537 in the paragraph "Man" in the *Instruction in Faith,* which read *recognoissance,* "acknowledgment." Man is to honor God with proper acknowledgment, that is, proper gratitude. Man is co-respondent, correspondent, to God, which ensures the lawful use of divine gifts. Else all is perverted.

> If we do not begin with this point—calling upon our God—then we pervert all *order.* So then let us learn that the principal exercise and study that the faithful ought to have in this world is to run to their God and, while acknowledging that he is the fountain of all blessings, seek good in him.[7]

> According as God continues to bless us, ought there not for this reason be a correspondence from our side [*correspondance de nostre costé*] so that we with perseverance pay homage to him for all his blessings?[8]

2. The Inverted Order of Creation

But, alas, paradise is lost; nor is this ideal or symbolic order often realized. Contrasted with this proper pattern of existence is the *inverted* order of creation (*inversus,* or *eversus creationis ordo*). Sin has dis-ordered this divine order of grace, brought "monstrous disorder." Calvin explains, "In the defection of the first man . . . the whole order of creation was everted"[9]—a statement which forms a recurring theme in his writings, and roughly parallels what a renovated Calvinism was to describe a century later as the breaking of the covenant of works. But this breach of order is a disruption of man's correspondence in grace. This occurs when men do not receive the whole of their felicity as a gift but ascribe it in part to endeavor of their own. "The order that he instituted at the creation of the world is troubled when he does not deal with us as a father."[10]

But that we live in an inverted order of creation never means for Calvin that God's purposes have been altered. Sin does not change God's gracious design. That remains regardless of the action of man. If it were not for the barrier of sin, God's original goodness would yet be showered upon us. Evils arise as man inverts and shuts off the God-given order. So Calvin insists:

> The Celestial Creator himself, however corrupted man may be, still keeps in view the end of his original creation . . .[11]

> Although we have for a time annihilated as much as is in us the graces of God, yet all the while he on his side does not wish that they should perish but he wishes to make them prosper.[12]

Calvin's position on natural theology has to be understood in terms of this original order of grace which God maintains while man perverts it. Were it not for sin, the natural man would live surrounded by "the mercy of the Lord," as the Psalmist (Ps. 33) exclaims. If men hunger or mourn, says Calvin,

> I answer that this happens contrary to the order of nature: namely, when the Lord on account of the sins of men closes his hand. For the liberality of God would constantly flow to us of its own accord . . . except that the obstacles of our sins shut it off.[13]

God does punish and discipline sinful men with natural evils. But these things happen contrary to the order of nature he for his part would have, as he is obliged to transform his world to expostulate with the ingratitude of man.

> These two things are then both true,—that God is not with-
> out a testimony as to his beneficence, for he gives rain, he gives
> suitable seasons, he renders the earth fruitful, so as to supply us
> with food,—and also, that heaven and earth are often in great
> *disorder,* that many things happen unseasonably, as though God
> had no care for us, because we provoke him by our sins, and
> thus *confound and subvert the order of nature.* These two things
> then ought to be viewed as connected together: for in the ordinary
> course of nature we may see the inconceivable bounty of God
> towards mankind; but as to *accidental* evils, the cause ought to be
> considered, even this—because we do not allow God to govern
> the world in a regular and consistent order . . .[14]

Originally, and yet ideally, man is to encounter and respond
to a gracious father God in an Eden earth. We press this point,
for here Calvin parallels what his successors were to term a general covenant made with all men.

> The right order of things was assuredly this, that man, contemplat-
> ing the wisdom of God in his works, by the light of the under-
> standing furnished him by nature, might arrive at an acquaint-
> ance with him.[15]

> Certainly all this [the works of God] should abundantly teach
> us all of such a God as it is necessary to know, if we in our
> coarseness were not blind to such a great light.[16]

The self-declaration of God is potentially complete. We could learn
about "his *mercy* which endures our iniquities with such a great
kindliness in order to call us to amendment."[17] "Displayed both in
heaven and on earth" are "clemency, goodness, mercy, righteousness, judgment, and truth." Psalm 145, Calvin argues in the *Institutes,* "contains such an accurate summary of all his perfections, that
nothing seems to be omitted. And yet it contains nothing but
what may be known from a contemplation of the creatures";
specifically it teaches us of his "mercy, in which alone consists all
our salvation."[18] The problem with the knowledge of God in the
natural order is not, as later Reformed thought was to say, its partial nature, or its inadequacy to fallen man. The problem is that
man ignores it. We return to this in chapter 7.

Though our perversity and unbelief cut off and disrupt both
natural and spiritual gifts, God's original gracious order has not
been rescinded; rather sin restricts and mars God's design and

wish. Passages such as the following abound in Calvin's commentaries and sermons:

> Unbelief blocks God from approaching us, and keeps as it were his hand shut. . . . Not that the power of God is bound by the inclination of men, but because, as far as they can, the obstacle of their malice shuts off that power, and they are unworthy that it should be laid open to them. . . . As often as he withdraws his hand so as not to assist unbelievers, this is done for this reason: that they, shut up within the narrow limits of their infidelity, do not allow it to enter.[19]

> God . . . deals very bountifully with the unbelieving, but they are blind; and hence he pours forth his grace without any benefit, as though he rained on flint or on arid rocks. However bountifully then God may bestow his grace on the unbelieving, they yet render his favour useless, for they are like stones.[20]

Man from his side manufactures sin out of God's grace. God's blessings "through accident" (*per accidens*) turn to our harm. As man refuses to acknowledge in response the gifts of God's grace, but rather arrogates them to his own use, they are prostituted, or transmuted to evil. Passages such as the following can be found by the hundreds in Calvin's sermons and commentaries:

> God has *ordered* his creatures for our service, and these ought to be a help to guide us to him so that we should be the more incited to love him because he shows himself a good and loving father to us, yet we take occasion at this to stumble. It is as though he should set up a ladder for us, or make stairs to come up on; and we happen to hurt ourselves by bumping against them. Stairs are made to help us, but if a man happens to fling himself against the stairs, he may happen to break his leg and hurt himself, and he shall rather be hindered than helped by them. So it is with us. God wishes to draw us to him by his creatures, and we happen to fling ourselves aginst them rashly and as it were in spite.[21]

> In all things and by every means he causes us now to taste his fatherly love with the intent that we might be confirmed in that which he declares to us in the gospel, to know that he has reserved a better heritage for us, as for children whom he has adopted. All the creatures then ought to point us heavenward. Yet in fact we put everything in reverse, because we apply the creatures of God to our own lust in such a way that we are held down here below. *In short, as many helps as God has given us to draw us to him-*

self, these are to us so many hindrances to hold us back in this world.[22]

We disguise God's truth and convert it into a lie, or else so paint it over that it is put quite out of its own nature. . . . All the graces that were bestowed on us become as many records to make us guilty before God; and so long as we continue in our nature, we do but abuse the benefits which we have received and apply them to evil. And so you see that always our confusion increases by all the gifts which God has bestowed upon us.[23]

In his Commentary on Ezekiel, Calvin elaborates on this way in which man transforms good. Sin is wrought as man ascribes to himself in pride what is in fact the gracious gift of God. Then God must resist in man what was given in love. The figurative "beauty" of the Hebrew nation is a symbol of all God's gifts in grace to mankind.

This passage, then, is worthy of observation, where God reproves his ancient people for trusting in their beauty: because the figure signifies that *they drew their material for pride from the gifts which ought rather to lead them to piety;* for the gifts which we receive from God's hand ought to be invitations to gratitude: but we are puffed up by pride and luxury, so that we profane God's gifts, in which his glory ought to shine forth. . . . God gives all things abundantly, and upbraids not, as James says, (chap. i. 5;) that is, if we acknowledge that we owe all things to him, and thus devote and consecrate ourselves in obedience to his glory, with the blessings which he has bestowed upon us. But when God sees us impiously burying and profaning his gifts, and, through trusting in them, growing insolent, it is not surprising if he reproves us beyond what is customary. Hence we see that God assumes as it were another character, when he expostulates with us concerning our ingratitude; because he willingly acknowledges his gifts in us, and receives them as if they were our own; as we call that bread ours by which he nourishes us, although *it is compelled to change its nature as far as we are concerned. It always remains the same in itself; but I speak of external form. God therefore, as it were, transfigures himself, so as to reprove his own gifts, conferred for the purpose of our glorying only in him.*[24]

Perhaps the major credibility gap in our entire argument arises here. We have cited Calvin at risk of belaboring the point because the reader who knows Calvin only secondhand will find it difficult to take seriously this emphasis on a gracious God who loves all with a fatherly love, but who finds his grace *frustrated* by man's ingratitude. Nor is this without considerable basis in firsthand fact. This seems almost another theological climate to the strongly pre-destinarian Calvin whose God accomplishes his every purpose foreordained throughout all eternity. Frankly, Calvin's theological determinism is not satisfactory, especially as it is clouded by a "secret counsel" from which reprobation flows. The Reformer does undermine much of what he has to say about divine grace, and we have no zeal to defend him here. The sovereignty of God is won, but the victory is Pyrrhic; he has surrendered much of his credibility when he praises the grace of God.

Calvin can and does delight in setting forth at length the grace of God. And where God is not so known, man frustrates him. Yet nonetheless all is foreordained. Is this sheer inconsistency? Perhaps. But to be fair to Calvin we should be as sympathetic as we can to three constructions which he uses to relieve this tension, constructions which have for the most part been overlooked or dismissed by his critics.

1. Calvin borrows from scholasticism the concept of an apparent *double will* in God, making a distinction between the *will* (*voluntas*) and the *secret counsel* (*arcanum consilium*), a distinction which, for all its shortcomings, he hopes to use to maintain the claim that God wills life in grace for all. Meanwhile, his secret counsel elects some. Though as far as we can see, this is a double will, it is in fact single in the heart of God. Calvin's critics counter, not without considerable force, that this makes God act with duplicity; but Calvin, at any rate, thinks not, and argues that paradoxical though these sometimes are, both the general will and the secret counsel flow from the grace of God. Calvin's most elaborate accounts of this are found in comment on Ezekiel 18, where God says, "I have no pleasure in the death of anyone," and on 1 Timothy 2, where God "desires all men to be saved." Listen to him as he preaches on the latter text:

> The Scripture does speak to us *doubly* [*doublement*] of the will of God. How so? Since God is not double, since there is no dissimulation at all in him, why is it that there is a double fashion of speaking about his will? It is because of our rudeness. For we know that God must transfigure himself in order to condescend

to us. . . . Scripture speaks of the will of God in two ways, not at all because this will is double, but because he must accommodate himself to our weakness. . . . When the Scripture tells us that God has chosen such as it pleased him before the creation of the world, this is a *secret counsel* into which we cannot enter. . . . But there is besides that the *will* of God which is open to us, such a will as he declares to us just as often as his word is preached to us. . . . From this we may judge that it is the will of God that all men should be saved.[25]

If we had leisure, we could follow this at length through hundreds of such passages. Perhaps the most unabashedly paradoxical are in Calvin's sermons and commentaries; yet even in his intensive treatment of providence in the *Institutes,* where Calvin strives for coherence and rationality, he rests his case with a bold paradox. "In a wonderful and ineffable manner, that is not done without his will which is yet contrary to his will . . ."[26] The supreme example is the death of Christ, crucified by evil men, yet foreordained to die by the counsel of God. But every sin is like that. The plain will of God, his precept, proscribes sin and prescribes life for all. Let us, insists Calvin, work and pray to that end. Hence his evangelistic energies. Hence Calvin is a universalist in his prayers. From this viewpoint, the chapter "Of the Gospel" ("Of the Gospel of the Love of God and Missions") added to the Confession in this century by the United Presbyterian Church and also by the Presbyterian Church, U.S., is unreservedly in the mood of Calvin, for all its tension with the eternal decrees of chapter III.

2. Calvin describes twofold causes which operate with asymmetry or imparity. These are variously termed *proximate* and *remote* causes, or *evident* and *hidden* causes. However logically problematic, it is consistent with our religious experience that in sin one does not need to look afar to some hidden cause in God. There is an evident cause near enough.

> I teach that a man ought to search for the cause of his condemnation in his corrupt nature rather than in the predestination of God. . . . I expressly state that there are two causes: the one *hidden* in the eternal counsel of God, and the other *manifest* in the sin of man. . . . Here then, *messieurs,* is the very core of the whole question: I say that all the reprobate will be convicted of guilt by their own conscience and that thus their condemnation

is righteous, and that they err in neglecting what is quite evident to enter instead into the secret counsel of God which to us is inaccessible.[27]

If Calvin sometimes elaborates this hidden cause so as to prejudice the reality of the nearer cause, he is not remaining true to his better insight.

3. God's grace has both *proper* (*proprium*) and also *accidental* (*accidentalis*) effects. To these we have already alluded. They may also be called *essential* and *adventitious* effects. Calvin is again borrowing from the scholastics, but his writings are so saturated with this distinction that *accident* develops into a technical concept for man's misuse and inversion of God's grace.

> When Christ says that he has come for judgment, when he is called a stone of offense, when he is said to be set for the ruin of many, this is *accidental,* or may be said to be *adventitious,* for they who reject the grace offered in him deserve to find him the judge and punisher of such unworthy and base contempt. The gospel gives us a striking example of this. For though it is *properly* the power of God to salvation to all who believe, yet the ingratitude of many causes it to turn into death for them.[28]

If even the gospel can be turned to our harm, how much more God's other gifts. Grace is resistible, if not ultimately, then surely penultimately. If words have meaning at all, we have to take Calvin seriously when he laments the frustrated grace of God.

> God would always be ready to relieve us by his goodness, or rather . . . it would flow down upon us as from a never-failing fountain, if our own ingratitude did not prevent or cut off its course.[29]

> Whenever we are deprived of the sense of God's favour, the way has been closed up through our fault; for God would ever be disposed willingly to show kindness, except our contumacy and hardness stood in the way.[30]

> *As then the moisture of rain does not penetrate into stones, so also the grace of God is spent in vain* [frustra] *and without advantage on the unbelieving.*[31]

A further point that must be balanced here is Calvin's use of the Augustinian notion of God's withdrawing the spiritual gifts after the fall. Sometimes he so states this as to question whether

God still wishes to give man the forfeited grace. "Man, since his fall, has been deprived of the gifts of grace on which salvation depends."[32] Taken in the larger context of his thought, it is clear that this withdrawal does not mean for Calvin that God no longer wills to be gracious to man in the order he once established. God has been obliged to punish man, yet this is not what God desires for man; creation is still so ordered objectively as to lead men to God and to eternal life. God has not removed his gifts so much as man has cut himself off from them. The whole apparatus through which these gifts were administered in nature remains in its entirety, inviting man to a knowledge of God's fatherly care. The gifts may be said to remain in this objective sense, though they never reach subjectivity in sinful man. In this sense, God still continues to give himself to man and so to impart spiritual gifts. They are properly said to be withdrawn only in that they are no longer subjectively realized.

That God has not deserted his order for man's life becomes again clear as he redeems man and re-establishes him in the original order of grace. Beginning right in the garden of Eden, grace superabounds, and God moves toward the covenant in which he chooses Israel in mission to the world and sends his Son to save the world. Redemption reveals that God has always willed to be gracious, still so wills, and is not finally going to let sin stand in his way. When God can no longer give life to man in the natural order, he does not break the order but reaffirms it in a new way as he enters history in his redemptive covenant.

> Whereas the Lord invites us to himself by means of the creatures with no effect . . . he has added, as was necessary, a new remedy, or rather a new aid, to assist our inept capacity.[33]

> As the whole world gained nothing in instruction from the fact that God had exhibited his wisdom in the creatures, he then resorted to another method for instructing man.[34]

It is important to see that when God's particular revelation in Israel and in Christ comes, this is a reaffirming of God's original order, and not—as later Reformed dogmatics interpreted it—the establishment of a new and different kind of order.

Though Calvin speaks extensively of the "special grace" involved in redemption, which has to be contrasted with a first, general grace, and though man immutably established in the new creation is more blessed than he was in the first, mutable paradise, the second creation is always essentially the same kind of order: the flowing out of God's grace to grateful man. Parallel to the two "orders" or covenants—works and grace—in the Westminster Confession, there is for Calvin but one order, order inverted, and order re-established. This involves a "new aid" or "another method," yet it is certainly not a new and contrasting order, but God's new way to establish and complete what he first instituted at creation. There is not the slightest suggestion in Calvin that God's grace appears in infralapsarian covenant with Abraham, fulfilled in Christ so as to contrast with and negate his earlier nongracious or semigracious ways, that grace is later showered upon a world previously and generally the realm of divine law. God's new way in Christ is in keeping with what has been the way of God from the beginning. The disorder that sin introduces is not the disruption of a prior and still determinative legal covenant; sin is first and everywhere the inversion and perversion of God's original and determinative ways of graciousness and goodness. Calvin's covenant of grace is in reflection of and in restoration of, not in contrast with, the original order. Calvin uses rarely the term "covenant of life," but this must not be confused with the "covenant of life" of the Westminster catechisms.[35] For him the covenant of life is synonymous with the one, gracious, redemptive covenant of God.

3. Grace and Law, and Vice Versa

We showed in the preceding chapter the long reach across Reformed thought of the primacy of law, flowing from the Westminster Confession's general legal covenant. The argument of this chapter is that the order of the Confession—law, law broken, then grace—was substituted for Calvin's grace, grace lost in ingratitude, and grace restored. In this contrasting of the covenant of works with Calvin's order of grace, it would be misleading to maintain that Calvin has no thought of law in his concept of the original relationship between God and man. But that place for law is clearly subordinate to grace.

The concept of law, of God's righteousness and from this

man's righteousness, is essential to divine order. It rightly has a vital place in God's ordering of his world. To that place we will turn in chapter 4. Order can be maintained only as man is obedient to divine law. But it would be inaccurate as well to set forth Calvin's concept of divine order principally along such terms. The principal thing in this first and fundamental order, the principle of it, is God's grace. Even though there are special graces which God later confers upon the elect when the broken order is re-established in redemption, God is father from the start. The world is ordered to demonstrate his paternal care in all man's needs, material and spiritual. From the very first, his will has ever been to sustain man by his grace alone.

It would be similarly inaccurate to maintain that covenant theology has no thought of grace in its concept of the first, legal covenant relationship between God and man. A limited kind of grace is required even for a covenant of works. The Westminster Confession nowhere specifies that this relationship is gracious, though it indicates that it is good and the result of divine "condescension." Cocceius speaks, however, of the "spiritual grace given him [Adam] at creation."[36] When thinking carefully at this point, Calvinism has usually remembered to say that an "aid of grace"[37] was needed by Adam if he were to persevere. Such a statement is dutifully included, almost as if covenant theologians were uneasy about forgetting something important. A. A. Hodge, son of Charles Hodge, makes this promising statement:

> This [legal] covenant was also in its essence a covenant of grace, in that it graciously promised life in the society of God as the freely-granted reward of an obedience already unconditionally due. Nevertheless it was a covenant of works and of law with respect to its demands and conditions.[38]

In this respect the treatment of R. L. Dabney is among the most satisfying; he speaks somewhat antithetically of a "gracious covenant of works."[39] In a recent interpretation of the Confession for contemporary Presbyterians, *The Westminster Confession for Today,* noting that the "notion of a covenant of works is one of the more controversial elements of the Federal theology," having very tenuous support in Scripture, Dr. George Hendry illustrates the most charitable and somewhat apologetic interpretation that can be put upon the contrasting covenants:

> God does not begin to be gracious when he makes the covenant of grace, as it is called; but it is now that the full depth of his grace, which is present in all his dealings with man, comes to light.[40]

But it is of serious consequence that such careful disclaimers and apologies always have to be made. Having reserved theoretically sufficient place for God to be gracious and having supposedly erected adequate safeguards, covenant theology always in fact returned by way of an eclipsing "nevertheless" (Hodge) to expound and operate with the legal demands and conditions of this half-gracious God of the first covenant. The end result was the making of the first and most fundamental relationship between God and man legal, not gracious. One must read grace into the Westminster Confession's covenant of works; it is not really there to be read out of it. Calvinism failed to understand and retain Calvin's concept of the grace of God as primary even in this primal and general relation between God and man; very soon the principle of it was no longer grace, but law. This succinct statement closes Fisher's chapter on the covenant of works, a statement which is much closer to the general mood of federal theology than is Hendry's apology:

> "The law was Adam's lease when God made him tenant of Eden; the conditions of which bond when he kept not, he forfeited himself and all for us." God read a lecture of the law to him before he fell, to be a hedge to keep him in paradise; but when Adam would not keep within compass, this law is now become as the flaming sword at Eden's gate, to keep him and his posterity out.[41]

Therefore at a most vital point, in this governing principle, Calvin and the theology of the Westminster Confession are not just different; they are as opposed as grace and law. With the coming of the conjugate covenants, there has now crept into Reformed theology a concept of the primal relationship between God and man, and a corresponding statement of the ability and merit of man, that is not only absent from Calvin but alien to his thought. This double covenant fabric not only modifies, it reverses much of Calvin's thought about man's primal relationship to God.

All this talk of covenants and orders instituted with Adam has, of course, to be demythologized for the modern Christian. But after the symbols are broken, as well as before, those who take the Westminster Confession seriously will find it has running through it a dualism between law and grace to which Calvin would have strenuously objected. The substructure of the Confession is a *coincidentia oppositorum,* a junction of opposites in which God is seen as operating doubly in his encounters with men, now on the basis of law, now on the basis of grace, a double dealing which if not schizophrenic is at least polar and ever in paradoxical tension. By contrast, despite some reservations about the divine secret counsel, Calvin builds from the first on the primacy of the grace of God.

CHAPTER 3

Man: His Duty and His Sin

In the teaching of Calvin, the understanding of man is reflexive of the order of grace, but by the time we reach the Westminster Confession a century later, the concept of man has become reflexive of the covenant of works. There are extremely important
differences in these two conceptions of man, differences which af-
fect the whole course of theology, and—here is the insidious legacy
—differences which tend to remain even when formal adherence to
the covenant of works becomes archaic. Failing to follow Calvin's
development of God's original relationship to man as dynamic and
gracious, covenant theology could not interpret the nature of man
in terms of his living in, or spurning, that relationship. Instead, it
was restricted to an exposition of duty and of sin in legal and
moral terms, in correspondence to the general legal covenant which
we are all born under. To these fundamentally different ways of
understanding the life of man and what God requires of him we
now turn. We shall witness an amazing spectacle: what for Calvin
is man's chief sin is, by the time we reach the Westminster Confession, his chief duty!

1. Man's Life as Acknowledgment of Grace

The one word which occurs more often than any other in
contexts where Calvin is dwelling on what man has to do is the
word "acknowledge." We may take as typical and normative a statement in his commentary on the Genesis saga, an exegesis which
Calvin has also incorporated systematically into the *Institutes* when
he treats the nature and condition of man.

> Adam was admonished, that he could claim nothing for himself as
> if it were his own, in order that he might depend wholly upon the
> the Son of God, and might not seek life anywhere but in him. But

> . . . he, at the time when he possessed life in safety, had it only as deposited in the Word of God, and could not otherwise retain it, than by *acknowledging* that it was received from Him . . .[1]

However it is elaborated, the answer to the question about duty must be in keeping with this original charge to the representative man. Adam's assignment involved, positively, a receiving of the life communicated to him from the Word of God, a depending wholly on the Son of God, and a praising of God which acknowledges him as the source of life and goodness. Negatively, it included a careful claiming of nothing for himself as if it were his own, and a steadfast faithfulness not to look elsewhere than God for his life.

If we ask more specifically about the content of this acknowledgment, Calvin readily expands it. His outworking of man's duty is essentially in terms of four elements: faith, obedience, love, and gratitude. Though he is not rigorously systematic in listing these elements, as the following citations will show, similar expositions do recur with interesting regularity. This, for instance, is one of the opening questions of the Geneva Catechism of 1541.

> Q. What is the way to honor God aright?
> A. To honor God aright is to put our whole trust in him, to study to serve him in obeying his will, to invoke him in all our necessities, seeking our salvation and all good things at his hand, and finally to acknowledge both with heart and mouth that he is the lively fountain of all goodness.[2]

At the head of his exposition of the Ten Commandments in the *Institutes* there appears this rather carefully chosen statement of what God commands:

> Although the duties we owe to God are innumerable, yet they may not improperly be classed under four general heads—adoration, a necessary branch of which is the spiritual obedience of the conscience; trust; invocation; and thanksgiving.[3]

The element of gratitude concludes both citations and sets the tone for the whole. The second chapter of Book I of the *Institutes* discusses the "tendency of the knowledge of God" and amounts to a measured statement of the duty of man in his integrity. A careful reading of this chapter illustrates how for Calvin it is the duty of man, whether innocent or repentant sinner, to live by the grace of God, to be

> ... persuaded that he is the fountain of all good, and seek for none but in him. ... we should therefore learn to expect and supplicate all these things from him, and thankfully to acknowledge what he gives us. ... Our knowledge of God should rather tend, first, to teach us fear and reverence; and, secondly, to instruct us to implore all good at his hand, and to render him the praise of all that we receive.[4]

It is vital to realize that in such passages as these Calvin is speaking of the duty of man both fundamentally and universally, that is, apart from considerations of sin and redemption. Later Reformed theology would have been able to state the particular duty of the elect in this way. But for the first-generation Reformer these statements are equally applicable to Adam in his innocence and to mankind generically. A closer look at each of these elements of duty will be instructive in terms of our larger thesis.

1. "The true service of God begins with *faith*" is Calvin's conclusion to "the sum of heavenly wisdom" in his commentary on Psalm 78. This Calvin calls the "root of true piety," and it has to be contrasted with the "root of the defection" in unfaithful man.

> Faith, then, is the root of true piety. It teaches us to trust in and expect every blessing from God, and it frames us to yield obedience to him; while those who distrust him must necessarily be always murmuring and rebelling against him.[5]

Trust, one of the four general heads of duty, is a virtually equivalent term, having a similar etymology in Latin (*fides, fiducia*). Confidence in God's goodness leads to the exercise of faith as a dependence upon God and an invocation of him for all things. Calvin's statements of duty frequently include such words as *depend, expect, implore, supplicate,* making man's life a larger life of prayer. This facet is separated out as another head of duty above. Regardless of the precise classification, he repeatedly refers to dependence on God as the central thrust of man's movement toward God.

> The principal points [of the service of God] are that we put our whole trust in him, that we acknowledge that all our blessings

come from him, that we invoke him because of this trust, and that we render him the praise for all that which he bestows upon us.[6]

There is an important sense in which it is man's duty to let God do for him what he is tempted to do for himself. The thing that Adam in behalf of all was so carefully encouraged to do, and the thing that men find most difficult to do, is to let God be for them all in all, to ask him for and to receive from him all good things. While there is a duty to do things for God, an obeying of his will that must be wrought out in action in life, this comes after and because God has done for us. Adam was to live by "faith,"[7] and the symbolic trees in the garden were calculated to develop and increase faith. Presumably the faith of integral man would have been somewhat different or on another level from that required of fallen man. But in Calvin's description of Adam's normative obligation to his God, all these elements of faith are conspicuously present: trust in the goodness of God, a depending wholly upon the Word of God (or Son of God), obedience, and gratitude. In short, Adam, as symbol of man in his noble wholeness, had, not less than redeemed man, more to let God do for him than to do for God; as he lived so, he was a man of faith. The duty of primal man and of man generically is not different in essence from that of the elect in the church. It is at this point that Reformed theology is soon to go astray.

2. An "obedience of faith" flows from such trust. Obedience was therefore the duty of Adam and remains the duty of all. In the symbolism of the Genesis parable, the commendation of the one tree and the prohibition of the other were lessons in obedience.

> Let us recognize that the principal thing which we must pursue is to conform and devote ourselves to the obedience of faith, that is, that our life be entirely regulated by the Word of God.[8]

> Abstinence from the fruit of one tree was a kind of first lesson in obedience, that man might know he had a Director and Lord of his life, on whose will he ought to depend, and in whose commands he ought to acquiesce. And this, truly, is the only rule of living well and rationally, that men should exercise themselves in obeying God. ... our life will then be rightly ordered, if we obey God, and if his will be the regulator of all our affections.[9]

In his preface to the exposition of the commandments in the *Institutes,* Calvin remarks, following Augustine, that obedience is "the parent and guardian," or "the origin of all virtues."[10]

Several aspects of this obedience are significant, especially as we anticipate the subsequent course of Reformed thought. It is part of man's corresponding to the grace of God; Calvin speaks of it, therefore, even for man in integrity, as an obedience of faith. It is not particularly or primarily a legal obedience, certainly not in the way it became so a century later. In contexts where man's obedience, or lack of it, is under discussion, as, for example, the *Institutes,* I, ii, Calvin does not often use the word "law," nor refer to it, unless he is actually involved in some exposition of the Mosaic law. He is more accustomed to speak of obedience to God's will, or to his command, government, order, or rule. He may speak of submission to God's authority, or of legitimate worship, or of reverence and fear of God.

If the question is raised, of course, Calvin does not hesitate to teach that Adam was given a law. In his Commentary on Genesis, he defends this point against the contention that law is irrelevant for man in his nobility. Calvin is no antinomian regarding man's duty in integrity; neither is he a legalist. The normative man's duty was to a divine *law,* even though in expounding the Genesis stories Calvin prefers, as he states (quite remarkably, in view of federal thought), to speak of the ordering of life according to the *will* of God.[11] It is an obedience *to* the law, but not *of* the law; it is an obedience of faith. It flows from faith, is born of love and gratitude, and keeps the law in praise of a beneficent and paternal God. Adam's relationship to law was essentially the same as that of redeemed man.

But this is not a meritorious obedience. Calvin insists on this at great length. The commandment to partake of the symbolic tree of life does not mean that life is achieved through its proper use.

> He gave the tree of life its name, not because it could confer on man that life with which he had been previously endued, but in order that it might be a symbol and memorial of the life which he had received from God.[12]

Calvin thought of this obedience in a certain sense as a *condition*

of man's continuing to receive grace. "At the beginning Adam was
appointed to be lord of all, on this condition, that he should continue
in obedience to God."[13] The commandment respecting the symbolic tree of knowledge of good and evil is a "test of obedience."
Life is given only *as,* but not *because,* man obeys. Calvin explains:

> The promise which authorized him to expect eternal life, as long
> as he should eat of the tree of life, and, on the other hand, the dread-
> ful denunciation of death, as soon as he should taste of the tree of
> knowledge of good and evil, were calculated for the probation and
> exercise of his faith.[14]

The authorized expectation of life for eating from the one tree,
or the judgment of death for eating from the other, could be iso-
lated as an incipient covenant of works. But the full statement
makes it clear that life was not conditional upon obedience in any
meritorious way. The legendary tree of life was a figure of Christ
to come, a sacrament to lead man to "the knowledge of divine
grace," so designed

> . . . that man, as often as he tasted of the fruit of that tree, should
> remember whence he received his life, in order that he might ac-
> knowledge that he lives not by his own power, but by the kindness
> of God alone; and that life is not (as they commonly speak) an in-
> trinsic good, but proceeds from God.[15]

It subsequently becomes apparent that the slightest hint to the
contrary, permitting man in some part to earn his salvation, is
resisted by Calvin as the beginning of degeneration into sin.

3. *Adoration,* or *love of God,* is the first of the four general
heads of duty. Calvin calls this "the commencement of godliness."
There are two components. Positively, this love rises in response
to a knowledge of God's perfections. To know him as the author
of every blessing is to love him. The *Instruction in Faith* of 1537
opens:

> . . . we are all created in order that we may know the majesty of
> our Creator, that having known it, we may esteem it above all and
> honor it with all awe, love, and reverence. . . . It is necessary, there-
> fore, that the principal care and solicitude of our life be to seek God,
> to aspire to him with all the affection of our heart, and to repose no-
> where else but in him alone.[16]

In the statement of man's duty in integrity in the *Institutes,* Calvin defines piety in terms of love, and argues that true piety cannot be found where man serves a just and dreaded lawgiver. No man can rightly serve God until he loves him, and no man can love him who is unacquainted with his paternal grace.

> True piety consists rather in a pure and true zeal which loves God altogether as Father, and reveres him truly as Lord, embraces his [righteousness] and dreads to offend him more than to die.[17]

Notions of God which fall short of a sure persuasion of his goodness are inadequate and vain; they cannot engender the love in which God is rightly served.

Negatively, this love necessitates a denial of self and self-will. Man's affection must be away from self and toward God. In that it is Godward, it is the love of God; in that it is away from self, it is self-denial. This is in keeping with the recognition that the talents and excellences we possess are not ours intrinsically, but gifts. Adoration of God is man's acknowledgment seen in antithesis to the concupiscence and self-love of which, as we shall see, Calvin speaks so often in his understanding of sin.

> The principal service that God demands is that we love him. . . . Instead of our concupiscences [i.e., self-willed desires], which draw us here and there, we are to have this affection which overrules, namely, that we take more pleasure in giving ourselves to him.[18]

We shall presently question whether the theology of the Westminster Confession is convincingly able to retain this kind of love as the duty of man in integrity under the legalized scheme of the covenant of works, where God is specifically not yet known as father, and where his gifts are rewards made conditional upon man's self-willed and meritorious obedience.

4. In the listing of the heads of duty prefatory to rightly understanding the commandments, Calvin includes *thanksgiving.* He never tires of reminding man how this alone sets the proper tone for life. Each of the statements of duty to which we have already referred has indicated this gratitude either specifically or in equivalent language. One further passage, a lyrical one from the Sermons on Ephesians, must suffice.

The principal sacrifice that God requires is that men *acknowledge* his benefits, that they pay homage to him, and that then these should excite men to do their duty. . . . For why are we fed by his goodness, why in short does he as it were put out our eyes with the great number of benefits that he bestows upon us, unless it is to the end that we should yield some *acknowledgment* of them to him? For, as it is said in the Psalm, we can from our side bring no profit to him, rather he requires in exchange nothing other than this *act of thanksgiving,* as it is said in Psalm 116: "What shall I render unto the Lord for all the benefits which I have received from him, unless I take the cup of salvation at his hand and call upon his name?" This then is what we have to bring to God: that we confess ourselves bound to him for all things.[19]

Man's duty is thus at every step set in response to the grace of God. Far more than his law, before as well as after redemption, for man in integrity and generically, it is the overwhelming goodness of God that puts man under obligation. "When [God] has of his own accord, conferred upon us his favour, he immediately afterwards requires from us gratitude in return."[20]

2. Man's Life as Works Under Law

The Westminster Shorter Catechism begins in the spirit of Calvin (if not actually borrowing from the Geneva Catechism) with a deservedly memorable answer to its opening question:

Q. What is the chief end of man?
A. Man's chief end is to glorify God, and to enjoy him forever.

Such a beginning promises a close following of Calvin in answer to the question about the duty of man. But instead, the Westminster divines made normative for all subsequent Presbyterians a concept of duty radically different from that which Calvin had given the Reformed church. A little later in the Catechism (question 12), the task assigned man is stated another way:

When God had created man, he entered into a covenant of life with him, upon condition of perfect obedience; forbidding him to eat of the tree of the knowledge of good and evil, upon pain of death.

The shifting mood is yet too subtle for the catechumen to catch, for had not Calvin said that Adam was placed in Eden "on this condition, that he should continue in obedience to God"?

Radical differences are, however, soon apparent. Compare Calvin's statement, cited earlier, from the *Instruction in Faith,* where man gifted with God's favor has but to "honor him with proper gratitude," with the calculated and contractual assertion of the Westminster Confession:

> God gave to Adam a law, as a covenant of works, by which he bound him and all his posterity to personal, entire, exact, and perpetual obedience; promised life upon the fulfilling, and threatened death upon the breach of it; and endued him with power and ability to keep it.[21]

The introduction of the covenant of works now means that when the question is asked, What is man to do, it must be answered most fundamentally: works of the law. The polar covenants have locked Reformed anthropology into a concept of duty alien to Calvin.

Faith is the subsequent duty of the elect; but works is man's universal duty. The covenant of works and the covenant of grace differ in "the diverse duties prescribed to man, to wit, works or faith" (Turretin). If faith is preserved nominally also as integral man's duty, it is reinterpreted as a work more to the credit of man than in response to the goodness of God. Turretin deals with this at length:

> In the first covenant faith was required as a work and a part of the inherent righteousness to which life was promised. But in the second it is demanded, not as a work on account of which life is given, but as a mere instrument apprehending the righteousness of Christ. . . . In the one, faith was a *theological virtue from the strength of nature,* terminating in God, the Creator; in the other, faith is an evangelical condition, after the manner of supernatural grace, terminating in God, the Redeemer.

> The first [covenant] gave matter for glorying to man when he observed it, but the second excludes all glorying of man because founded upon the grace of God alone.[22]

Such faith is an index of man's strength, a meritorious theological virtue, and its mood is radically different from that faithful dependence on God alone which Calvin had prescribed for integral man.

Under the shadow of the covenant of works, the Reformer's "obedience of faith" becomes an "obedience of works" with worth and merit such as Calvin never assigned to it. Ames speaks for the Reformed consensus:

> That [covenant] required perfect *obedience of works,* which was to be performed by man with his own strength before the promise took any effect, in order that the covenant might take merit into account.[23]

Condition as used of the first covenant in the Westminster standards means something else from what it had meant to Calvin. The word "condition" is used in two senses, Hodge explains. It ought not in any sense be considered meritorious when used of faith and the second covenant. But it clearly does mean "meritorious consideration" when used of works in the first.

> In this sense [of a meritorious consideration] perfect obedience was the condition of the covenant originally made with Adam. Had he retained his integrity he would have merited the promised blessing. For to him that worketh the reward is not of grace but of debt.[24]

It is not difficult to find in the federal writers discussions of how the legendary innocent man was to delight in God's law and goodness, though mention of the grace or beneficence of God is typically absent at this stage. Supposedly, there is a certain high happiness in this legal obedience. But all this becomes peculiarly unsatisfying when we are told that this enjoying of God to which the Shorter Catechism refers is a formal, contractual duty of works. It seems now less a cause for rejoicing than a cause for forboding, for wondering whether man is able to accomplish the fearful task given him, and perhaps for wondering too whether God is really fair in what he so stringently asks of man in this transaction.

At once there is a twofold shift. First, there is little thought of God's goodness as putting man under obligation; duty is now defined in terms of law, because duty is derived from law. The catechumen is taught:

Q. What is the duty which God requireth of man?
A. The duty which God requireth of man is obedience to his re-

> vealed will. . . . The moral law is the declaration of the will of God
> to mankind, directing and binding everyone to personal, perfect,
> and perpetual conformity and obedience thereunto . . .[25]

Secondly, duty shifts to focus on man's initiative. The man who
in Calvin's thought was to seek and receive all good from the hand
of God, and thankfully to acknowledge it, has now to do for himself. What place is there for gratitude, when the burden of achiev-
ing life is laid so squarely on his own shoulders? Listen to Witsius:

> Such a perfect observance of the laws of the covenant . . . had given
> man a right to the reward. . . . he could say, I have fulfilled the
> conditions of the covenant, I have constantly and perfectly done
> what was commanded; now I claim and expect that thou, my God,
> wilt grant the promised happiness.[26]

There is a theoretical but ineffectual safeguard in the frequent
reservation that man's working is not intrinsically meritorious;
works have merit only within God's condescension to the legal
covenant. Despite these disclaimers, the clear emphasis is now on
man's working for himself.

This concept of duty is by no means academic or antiquated;
it is a duty which, according to the Westminster Confession and
the received Reformed anthropology, is ever in force as the duty
of the universal race of men. The covenant of works "has not
been abrogated as a duty and an obligation."[27] The Confession
can go on to state the duties of the elect under the covenant of
grace quite commensurably with the teaching of Calvin. Subsequently we receive by faith what we could not obtain by works;
then there is cause for trust, gratitude, and love. But we cannot
forget that the law of God stipulates a duty of works for all men;
the grace of God provides a new and special duty for believers.
A distorted concept of the nature of man in the foundations of the
federal system throws out of plumb the whole theological edifice
built upon it. The notion that basically works of the law compre-
hend the whole duty of man has cast a long shadow across the
church. Such a duty of man, remember, is not merely given a
mythical Adam. It is given us all. Each is born under it. That
heritage is difficult to escape both theologically and psychologically.

3. Sin as Man's Dis-grace

According to Calvin, in sin man dis-graces himself. The order of dependence on divine goodness is dis-ordered as man turns
to depend on himself. In this, man is a sinner not only as he is im-
moral or fails to conform to law. Rather he takes the rectitude
with which he was blessed and ascribes it to himself, thereby
making it a curse. He is dis-eased. By contrast, Reformed tradition since, having put little emphasis on the grace of God to man
in creation, has not understood sin as having this character. Instead,
federal thought was restricted to an exposition of sin in legal and
moral terms, in correspondence to the legal covenant which it
supposed God had at first instituted. Calvin and the Calvinists,
despite superficial similarities, have fundamentally different ways
of describing the fundamental sin.

Calvin speaks of the "root of the defection" or "source" or
"cause" of sin, by which he means the basic, original sin on which
rests the whole superstructure of sins. This sin of Adam, as representative man, is the recurring sin of all. Calvin's analysis of the
root sin is done from four basic viewpoints, in each case recog-
nizing that man has done precisely the opposite of that duty which
has been set out earlier in this chapter.

1. Calvin's most specific answer to the inquiry about the fundamental sin is *infidelity* or faithlessness (*infidelitas*). Emphasis
here is on man's unfaithful rejection of the grace of God as he
turned to look elsewhere for greater security and happiness. In
the *Institutes,* paralleled in the Commentary on Genesis, Calvin
writes of Adam's fabled crime:

> Since . . . it must have been a detestable crime, that was so severely
> punished by God, we must consider the nature of Adam's sin . . .
> Infidelity . . . was the root of that defection. But hence sprang am-
> bition, pride, and ingratitude, since Adam, by coveting more than
> was granted, offered an indignity to the Divine goodness, which
> had so greatly enriched him.[28]

> What was the sin of them both? . . . Infidelity was the root of the
> defection, just as faith alone unites us to God.[29]

Infidelity is not an opposite primarily of obedience, but rather of
trust. As faith was man's duty, conversely infidelity is his sin. It is

more of "an indignity to the divine goodness" than to the divine law. In the paragraph "Man" in the *Instruction in Faith,* duty and sin are clear opposites. Man was formed to honor God with proper gratitude.

> But, having trusted such a great excellence of his nature and having forgotten from whom it had come and by whom it subsisted, man strove to raise himself up apart from the Lord.

A closely related category is that of unbelief *(incredulitas)*:

> This is the source of all evils, when we are not fully convinced that in God is everything that can be desired for our salvation.[30]

> All evils arise from unbelief and distrust.[31]

2. But Calvin can speak freely of sin as *disobedience.* Here Calvin includes that facet of sin which tended to become the sole category of analysis in subsequent Reformed theology. In setting forth Calvin's broader concepts, we must not obscure the fact that sin as disobedience is one—but only one—of the elements of sin. In his treatment in the *Institutes* of the "nature of Adam's sin," Calvin cites the tree of knowledge as a symbolic "test of obedience" and describes the first sin as disobedience, as well as infidelity.

> As the woman, by the subtlety of the serpent, was seduced to discredit the word of God, it is evident that the fall commenced in disobedience. This is also confirmed by Paul, who states that all men were ruined by the disobedience of one. . . . the first man rebelled against the government of God, . . . despised the truth, and turned aside to falsehood.[32]

This disobedience is a fundamental overthrow of the order and government of God. It is not simply violation of law, but active rebellion. In the Genesis parable, Adam was not content with his dependent condition but wanted something higher—independence, or self-sufficiency. He did not want to be subject, but rather to be autonomous. His deed is illegal, but more: his deed is disgraceful.

3. The fundamental sin of man may also be analyzed as *concupiscence (concupiscentia).* By this Calvin emphasizes the self-willed and selfish aspects of man's continual revolt from God.

Concupiscence is basically self-love and the opposite of the love of God. God requires of man a grateful response in love, but man in concupiscence has loved himself and sought his own felicity. Adam "is tempted by his own concupiscence . . . and . . . not otherwise than knowingly and willingly, had set himself, as a rebel, against God." Similarly, it was the "poison of concupiscence"[33] that infected Eve. Concupiscence is the fountain and root of all sin, the inverting and corrupting power that permeates the whole of life.

> [Concupiscence] . . . is not any kind of evil affection or desire, but that which is the fountain of all evil affections . . .[34]

> Paul names this as the sin from which all sins proceed: concupiscence.[35]

A complicating factor is the use of "concupiscence" in various ways. *Concupiscentia* may mean a grosser vice, Calvin explains in a discussion of *lust* (Vulgate: *concupiscentia*) in 1 John 2:16.[36] But there is also a more fundamental, hidden form of concupiscence. All of the Greek virtues—justice, uprightness, moderation, prudence, fidelity—are rejected by Calvin because the natural man does not recognize his concupiscence in them. The keeping of the law, if done in self-will, is concupiscent. We may "agree with the law of God in regard to the mere outward actions" but be inwardly concupiscent. There is a *concupiscentia* which keeps the letter of the law (at least the first nine precepts) and is zealous for serving God.

Calvin is impressed by Paul's experience. The apostle writes in Romans 7, "I should not have known what concupiscence is if the law had not said: Thou shalt not covet [*non concupisces*]. While keeping the nine precepts, Paul was blind to the tenth; so interpreted, the law "indeed bridles our external actions, but does not in the least restrain the fury of our concupiscence." The final commandment goes beyond all the rest of forbidding desires which are autonomous.

> The sin of concupiscence is more secret and deeply hidden. For this reason men never take it into account, as long as they judge according to their own sense. . . . [Paul] was deceived during the time that he did not believe that his righteousness was hindered by his

concupiscence, yet he finally perceived that he was a sinner, when he saw that concupiscence, from which no human being is free, was proscribed by the law. Augustine says that Paul included the whole of the law in this expression. If rightly understood, this is true. . . .

God, however, in this precept goes to the heart of our concupiscence, which, because it is more concealed than the will, is not accounted a vice. Not only was it pardoned by the philosophers, but at the present time the papists fiercely maintain that in the regenerate it is not a sin. Paul, however, says that he had found the source of his sin in this hidden disease.[37]

Contemporary use of the term "self-will" is nearly synonymous with what Calvin is after here. Concupiscence is the opposite of conforming life to the will of God; it is the ἀταξία (disorder) which enters when man does not depend on God, but rather on himself. Paul had formally and sincerely kept the law, so he thought. Yet he was the concupiscent chief of sinners because of all men he most believed himself to have attained his own eternal life. His very self-reliance was but a subtle concupiscence. Paul's trouble was that "being puffed up with confidence in his own righteousness, he expected salvation by his works."[38] Of all men's concupiscent desires, here is the worst:

Whenever our minds are pestered with this cupidity, to desire to have something of our own, which may reside in ourselves rather than in God, we may know that this idea is suggested by the same counsellor, who excited in our first parents the desire of resembling "gods, knowing good and evil."[39]

Here the bearing of Calvin's understanding of concupiscence on our study becomes clear. Not only did the philosophers and the "papists" fiercely maintain that there is a legitimate place for autonomous desires through which man earns his own righteousness, so also did the Westminster divines—not practically, of course, so far they differed, but theoretically. In the duty they assigned to man generically and in integrity, philosopher, papist, and Westminster divine were in full accord.

4. A final, most basic way of describing the primal sin is in terms of *ingratitude*. When God had enriched Adam with bounteous gifts, he lost all through ingratitude. This theme underlies the opening paragraph of a significant chapter in the *Institutes* (II, ii),

and it is extensively developed in Calvin's sermons, notably on Deuteronomy and Job:

> God was not niggardly in his blessings, but poured them out bountifully, just as he who is the fountain of all liberality. He showed himself more than liberal toward mankind in the person of Adam. But we lost those blessings, God had to curtail his blessings which he had given us, because Adam through his ingratitude became corrupted.[40]

> Adam could not abide all that, and by his ingratitude he alienated himself from God.[41]

This theme is found in Paul's opening chapters in Romans. Though all have not had the legendary felicity of Adam, yet all have had or ignored blessings in abundance, and from this their sin arises.

> Man's nature universally contains the seed of all evils . . . Thus Paul, in the first chapter of his Epistle to the Romans, piles up many different kinds of vices and crimes, which flow from ignorance of God, and that ingratitude, of which he had shown all unbelievers to be guilty . . .[42]

Calvin thought of sin in its broad dimensions by choosing a number of fluid concepts which revolve around the single insight of sin as man's dis-gracing himself in self-will. In each of these ways of thinking about the primal sin—infidelity, disobedience, concupiscence and self-will, and ingratitude—Calvin keeps in constant focus the breaking of the original order of grace. Sin has to be set opposite the love of God as man's refusal to be loved by God and his desire to love himself.

4. Sin as Transgression of Law

When one lays aside Calvin to search the Calvinists for the nature of sin, he comes into a much smaller world. The simple, almost exclusive definition is that sin is breaking the law. Covenant theology can rise no further than the classic answer of the Westminster Shorter Catechism, a memorable reply which, on account of its half-truth, has done as much ill as good in Reformed thought.

> Sin is any want of conformity unto, or transgression of, the law of God.[43]

This definition represents the settled consensus of orthodoxy, held with alarming tenacity. One wonders that covenant theologians could speak at all of a "fall from grace," for there is little concept of any fall from any grace in their analysis of sin. Exclusively now it is a development of the breaking of the covenant of works. Adam's sin, and hence the generic sin of man, is in essence a legal transgression.

> This act of his was a wilful transgression of a law, under the precepts whereof he was most justly created; and under the malediction whereof he was as necessarily and righteously subject. . . . Though at first glance it seems to be a small offence, yet, if we look more earnestly upon the matter it will appear to be an exceeding great offence . . . Nay, how could there be a greater sin committed than that, when Adam, at that one clap, broke all the ten commandments?[44]

Many writers prove that Adam broke both tables of the law; some demonstrate how he broke each one of the ten commandments.

The *locus classicus* in Scripture is 1 John 3:4: "sin is lawlessness." The Greek here is ἀνομία, a combination of α (without) and νόμος (law). In his commentary here Calvin had noticed, somewhat incidentally, John's defining sin as the transgression of the law, though it is significant that reference to 1 John 3:4 does not occur in the *Institutes*. Now lawlessness becomes the definitive concept. Even the word infatuates and is taken over intact, often untranslated, and employed in virtually every federal definition of sin.

> [Sin's] nature is clearly shown by the apostle, when he says, "Sin is the transgression of the law". . . The essence of sin therefore consists in a contrariety to the divine law, and it is the absence of that rectitude, which ought to be in a rational creature according to the requirement of that law. Hence in order to ascertain whether any thing is sinful, we must examine whether it is contrary to the law; for nothing else is required.[45]

> The form or formal nature of sin is deformity, i.e., aberration from the divine law, ἀνομία. Accordingly, sin is nothing else but what is committed against the law of God.[46]

Wider categories, such as those Calvin had used, may still be present, though they are conspicuously absent from many writers. Turretin's answer to the question about the first sin is, in a superficial way, much like Calvin's. Adam's sin was an aggregate of many. Turretin makes a place for pride, disobedience, concupiscence, unbelief, distrust, and even—which is rare in the covenant theologians—ingratitude. But everything now falls under the shadow of the covenant of works. Most fundamentally, Adam broke the law, both tables of it. He "transgressed . . . the whole law of nature engraved upon his heart." For all the similarities to Calvin, there is in Turretin a pronounced emphasis on law foreign to his predecessor in Geneva.

> It is certain that we must not regard that fall as any particular sin, such as theft, or adultery, but as a general apostasy and defection from God, a violation not only of the special positive law about not eating the forbidden fruit, but also of the whole moral law, included in it, and so also of the obedience, which man owed to God, his Creator, especially by reason of the covenant entered into with him: so that here is, as it were, a complicated disease, and a total aggregate of various acts, both internal and external, impinging against both tables of the law. For as by unbelief and contempt of the divine word, ingratitude, pride, and profanation of the divine name, he transgressed the first table, so the second, by want of affection toward children, by homicide, precipitating himself and children into death, by intemperance, and gluttony, theft, and appropriation of another's property without his consent, unlawful love, and depraved concupiscence.[47]

These other elements are fitted into it, but the first sin was essentially a legal transgression. Witsius speaks in the mood of the Westminster divines:

> In that sin, as divines generally observe, there was, as it were, a kind of complication of many crimes. But it is our chief purpose to show that this was the violation of the whole covenant [of works]; . . . the covenant in its whole constitution was violated by that transgression: *the law* of the covenant was trampled upon . . .[48]

When the covenant writers speak of the symbolic unbelief of Adam, they note that this is a legal unbelief. Indeed, so thoroughly does sin become reflexive of law that many federal exponents adopt the curious and remarkable argument that there is no sin against the covenant of grace, only against the first covenant; correspondingly, all judgment and justice flows from the first covenant, none from the second. There are no evangelical sins, only legal transgressions. Witsius may again serve as their spokesman:

> The covenant of grace has no threatenings . . . peculiar to itself, but what may well be referred to the law, from which every curse proceeds. . . . As, therefore, unbelief, or the rejecting the Gospel, is a sin against the law, which is the only perfect rule of all virtue (it can be called a sin against the Gospel, only objectively), so every threatening of the curse and of wrath against unbelievers and the despisers of the Gospel, must come from and be reduced to the law . . .[49]

All man's unfaithfulness and infidelity and disobedience is apostasy from law, and concupiscence is defined as "the propension of all the forces to do that is prohibited by the law of God."[50] That all this flagrantly distorts Calvin is readily evidenced by the observation that, in his principal chapter on sin in the *Institutes*, II, i, Calvin often speaks of man's disobedience under "the government of God," but he does not here directly refer to the law of God at all![51]

The most radical consequence of the now legalized doctrine of sin is that covenant theology does not, for indeed it cannot, describe sin in what is for Calvin the most basic way of all: man's faithless rejection of the goodness of God in favor of his self-willed efforts to seek his own happiness elsewhere. Here Calvin and the Calvinists come at length to a parting of the ways. When Calvin describes sin as that faithlessness which cuts off God's grace, he has gone where none of the Westminster divines can follow. They can only go further along their own way of describing sin as lawlessness, because, with the intervention of the covenant of works, they know nothing about man's first duty as that of faithfulness to depend on divine goodness. And before the end of the way is reached, these paths of Calvin and his followers are not simply parted but are opposed. Repeatedly, and at significant points in his writings, where Calvin is putting the whole thing in perspective (*Institutes*, II, ii, 10; Commentary on Genesis, chapter 2; *Instruction in Faith*), we have heard Calvin warn against "this cupidity, to desire to have something of our own, which may reside in ourselves rather than in God," this failure of man to be grateful for grace, and this seeking of man "to raise himself up apart from the Lord." For man this desire for recognition, for something in which to boast, is the beginning of the end.

The coming of the covenant of works permits what Calvin forbids. It prescribes for man just what Calvin proscribes: the attempt to rely on something of man's own and not to seek life as the gift of God. We have heard Calvin say in his exposition of the Genesis myth that Adam, the representative man, cannot claim any virtue for his own:

> Adam was admonished, that he could claim nothing for himself as if it were his own, in order that he might depend wholly upon the Son of God, and might not seek life anywhere but in him. But . . . he, at the time when he possessed life in safety, had it only as deposited in the Word of God, and could not otherwise retain it, than by acknowledging that it was received from Him . . .[52]

But this is the very thing that the theology of the Westminster Confession now encourages man to do. Witsius explains that under the general, universal covenant a place is allotted and permitted for man to have a "boasting" and a "glorying" of his own.

> In the covenant of works, man is considered as working, and the reward to be given as of debt; and therefore, man's glorying is not excluded, but he may glory, as a faithful servant may do, upon the right discharge of his duty, and may claim the reward promised to his working.[53]

Here, at the end of the way, Reformed confessional orthodoxy is walking a path alien to Calvin. It does not know that in the very positing of such a boasting for man, integral man or not, sin is latent; indeed, here is the chief sin of man.

CHAPTER 4

Law in Covenant and Nature

It has very often been observed that by the time one reaches the Westminster Confession, Reformed orthodoxy has fallen into a legalism that is wholly uncharacteristic of the Reformer himself. The Confession of Faith reads like a constitution; the Westminster divines wrote like lawyers. We have seen how this new legalism recast and reversed Calvin's understanding of man, his duty, and his sin. Our argument can now best be pursued by turning to an analysis of the whole place of law in the theological system of Calvin, to see, first, how Calvin avoided this legalism and, second, how and where those who supposed themselves to be his followers veered off into a radically different use of law. Law is doubly manifested, in Scripture and in nature; our account must be twofold.

1. The Law of Moses and Its Place in the Covenant

For Calvin there is but one covenant, beginning at creation and continuing now and ever. "All those persons, from the beginning of the world, whom God has adopted into the society of his people, have been in covenant [*foederatus*] bound to him by the same law and doctrine which are in force among us."[1] But this gracious covenant falls "under shadows" in the Old Testament period; in substance it is the same, but different in administration. Under Moses, the law is given as a schoolmaster to teach of the Abrahamic covenant and to point to Christ. Calvin's several pedagogic uses of law reduce to two. The "principal" and "proper" use of law is as a pattern for the life of gratitude.[2] Calvin dwells on this at length, but the second use of law is of more importance for our theme, as it reveals both the fundamental subordination of law to grace and the point where Calvinists later reversed this subordination.

When the covenant of grace falls under shadows, God "recedes from the strictness of his claims" and makes what Calvin calls a *legal promise,* as distinct from an *evangelical promise.* At this point (and at this point only) in Calvin's thought we have a righteousness of works somewhat suggestive of what was to be formalized in the Westminster Confession as a covenant of works:

> Since the eyes of our mind are too dim to be attracted with the mere beauty of virtue, our most merciful Father has been graciously pleased to allure us to the love and worship of himself by the sweetness of his rewards. He announces, therefore, that he has reserved rewards for virtue, and that the person who obeys his commandments shall not labour in vain.[3]

> Such promises . . . proclaim that a reward is ready to be bestowed, on condition that we perform what is commanded.[4]

For those blinded to grace, fallen from integrity, diseased by sin (a quite opposite condition from that for which the Westminster Confession proposes the covenant of works), God lays aside the original, gracious order of things, and even more graciously "recedes" to propose a legal righteousness. That he so permits abuse of the proper order is, note, a sign of his mercy. Law appears when grace fails, and not, as the Calvinists would have it, vice versa. The Sermons on Galatians are Calvin's best exposition of law. A paragraph well illustrates the tenor of this approach.

> Men have always deluded themselves with vainglory and presumption that they could purchase salvation. Therefore God has to say to them, Go to, if you are such able men as you think, show it. As for me, I will let you have my law, and so that you will not think yourselves ill dealt with for your serving me, your salary is ready for you if you perform it. There it is; eternal life is definitely assured to you. But now let us see a little what you can do. Busy yourselves to your work![5]

God's intent, of course, is otherwise than his offer; or perhaps more accurately, it is larger than his offer. His purpose is to lead through law to grace. In failure, man may see his sin and be driven through despair to grace.

This righteousness of works is an attachment to the one covenant of grace, when it falls under shadows. While Calvin may say that "God enters into covenant with us, and, so to speak, brings himself under obligation to recompense our obedience,"[6] there is certainly no idea of God's returning to and restating for any purpose whatever any first and primitive legal covenant. This is a gracious covenant, darkened by the shadows of sin. Calvin is ever apologetic about this righteousness of the law so as to reduce any emphasis on even a theoretical merit of works. Witness again the Sermons on Galatians:

> Although we had angelic perfection, yet that could not obligate God to us at all, if it were not that he of his own good will had given this promise in his law: He that does these things shall live by them. Then if we attempt to acquire grace from God by our own works, we must not argue as does philosophy that God owes us wages or recompense for the service that we have done him. For we are his and cannot bind him by anything that we could do.
>
> How then is it that our works could be recompensed as though they were meritorious before God? Because he has promised so to do. It is the covenant which he has made with us, saying: He that does these things shall live by them. So then, if we could perform the law in its perfection, surely we should be righteous before God and merit salvation; not for any worthiness that should be in ourselves, however, but by reason of the covenant that God has made with us. For we see that all the desert which could be alleged from the side of man depends wholly upon this promise.[7]

The legal promise is made, not strictly, but just the opposite, as God "recedes from the strictness of his claims." It belongs *ex pacto,* i.e., in the context of the covenant of grace, but dimly seen. It is essentially God's way of driving man deeper into his own self-willed corruption in order that, made worse, he may later be bettered.

But Calvin's account is not without some problems. Though he holds that God's objective in the law is to reduce man to grace, yet Calvin thinks of this condemnation, inevitably involved, as a "contrary effect of the law." God purposed it so, but it is also an *accidental* or *adventitious* effect, which with Calvin usually implies that it was not God's purpose.[8] Calvin's reply would probably be that, wrestling with sin, God foresees and makes beneficial use of even this contrary effect of law.

A more serious problem is whether, if sin is more than legal transgression, the law can fully reveal sin. Calvin's theological orientation, as we have sketched it, indicates that sin can be fully known only reflexively of grace. Is the law, conceived as a legal promise, adequate to show man his deepest sin? Calvin knows that it is not. Law reveals sin clearly, dramatically, yet also to a certain extent partially. Only the gospel fully uncovers sin. He raises the point in commenting on Hebrews 4:12, where the word of God is a sword revealing the wickedness of man. Is this word law or gospel? In part both, answers Calvin, but especially the gospel:

> As it is Christ's office to uncover and bring to light the thoughts from the recesses of the heart, this he does for the most part by the Gospel.[9]

Consistently with his total position, Calvin can say emphatically that grace reveals sin as law cannot. We turn once again to the Sermons on Galatians:

> We must always return to this principle which we have treated, namely, that in the gospel we are completely stripped of all the goodness and virtue which we thought ourselves to have, and that God makes us so ashamed that we are obliged to come to him as quite confounded. Because *although God sets our cursedness before us in the law, yet we perceive it not so well there as in the gospel.*[10]

But frankly also, Calvin sometimes forgets this, and in his extensive use of Paul's "by the law is the knowledge of sin," it may fairly be said that Calvin does not always add the unique word about sin that only grace can teach. Weakness or carelessness here has quite possibly allowed the federal theology of a later age to seem at home in Calvin. He may assign to law the particular office of revealing sin, played in contradistinction to the saving role of grace.

> It is not the gospel which has condemned me, it is not the gospel that has showed me my filthiness, to make me ashamed of it; it is not the gospel which has bereft me of all hope of salvation, but it is the law which has showed me that I am dead, that I am damnable before God, that I am damned and lost. This comes from nowhere else than from the law.[11]

One who had heard Calvin preach so, and heard no more, could be excused for resting content with the Shorter Catechism's simplistic definition of sin as transgression of law.

Significantly though, while Calvin speaks often of the uncovering of sin by law, he never defines sin in terms of law. Logically or theologically, the knowledge of sin follows the knowledge of grace, but experientially—pedagogically, psychologically—it follows the knowledge of law. Why was the Mosaic law added to the Abrahamic covenant? According to a passage from the Sermons on Galatians, to teach men of sin—a thing, moreover, which by all theory the gracious covenant ought to have done, yet practically it had not.

> The law was added to make men know that God has rightly condemned them all. . . . Now if it is argued that the promise ought to have served to do that, the answer and solution is easy. . . . It is true that this ought to make us perceive our miseries and be sorry for them, but we are so fast asleep in our sins that we never think about them unless we are forced. Although, then, after God gave the promise to them, men should have had occasion to lament their sins, to the end that they might rest themselves wholly on the grace of our Lord Jesus Christ, yet they did it not at all until God had struck them as with many blows of a hammer, which he has done by the law.[12]

Law awakens man to sin. Yet law cannot teach of the deepest sin. By Calvin's fullest account, man's works under law are sinful not merely because they are imperfect, but also because they are legal.

2. The Law of Moses and the Covenant of Works

Fisher appeals to the Reformer as he writes, and he does seem superficially to reproduce Calvin on the law:

> But God knew well enough that the Israelites were never able to yield such an obedience: and yet he saw it meet to propound eternal life to them upon these terms; that so he might speak to them in their own humour, as indeed it was meet: for they swelled with mad assurance in themselves, saying, "All that the Lord commandeth we will do," and be obedient, Exod. xix. 8. Well, said the Lord, if you will needs be doing, why here is a law to be kept; and if you can fully observe the righteousness of it, you shall be saved . . .[13]

They concur that God gave law at Sinai to uncover sin and to lead to grace. But this togetherness is deceptive; there are differences beneath of great theological moment.

The giving of the law is for covenant theology a return to the covenant of works, set now within and mixed with the covenant of grace. It is a return for a different purpose, now to lead man from law to grace, but a return nonetheless. The Westminster Confession is perfectly clear on this point:

> God gave to Adam a law, as a covenant of works . . . This law, after his fall, continued to be a perfect rule of righteousness; and, as such, was delivered by God upon mount Sinai in ten commandments . . .[14]

Covenant writers spent much labor on and differ somewhat in the details of the mixing of the two covenants. But they hold this in common: that Mosaic law in some sense involved a restatement of the normative covenant, to which there must be at least some returning, as only from this contract does man learn his duty, his sin, and the judgment under which he stands. So argue Turretin and Fisher:

> It was . . . a new economy of the covenant of grace . . . clothed as to external dispensation with the form of a covenant of works, through the harsh promulgation of the law, and not indeed with that design, so that a covenant of works might again be demanded with the sinner; for this were impossible; but that a daily recollection and reproaching of the violated covenant of works might be made.[15]

> So that you see the Lord's intention therein was, that they, by looking upon this covenant might be put in mind what was their duty of old, when they were in Adam's loins; yea, and what was their duty still, if they would stand to that covenant, and so go the old and natural way to work; yea, and hereby they were also to see what was their present infirmity in not doing their duty: that so they seeing an impossibility of obtaining life by that way of works, first appointed in paradise, they might be humbled, and more heedfully mind the promise made to their father Abraham . . .[16]

Beneath the superficial similarity there has occurred a deep shifting of presuppositions. In Calvin, the law is superadded to the covenant of grace. So far as it is a legal promise, and therefore so far as it resembles a covenant of works, it is given for the first time at Sinai as God yields to the stubbornness of sin. Even there, "properly" understood it is a pattern of response for the life of grace. But it is widely "improperly" understood, and God makes cathartic use of this misunderstanding. He lets law be dimmed and diffracted through the sinfulness of men. Men are wont so to work for salvation that God lets them have a try at it. But in the Westminster Confession, law is not really so much added to grace, as is grace added to law. Law is added, but the adding is by way of reminder of the universal legal covenant which has gone before and which has perpetual validity. That which is really prior at Sinai is law. God in legal covenant recalls to man the order instituted at creation and reiterates the original terms of salvation. This primal and ever continuing "perfect rule of righteousness" precedes, parallels, and in a real sense determines the schema of things into which the second, gracious way of righteousness must be fitted.

From the viewpoint of Calvin, when God gives law, he is certainly not returning to the natural and ideal way of righteousness for which he created man; quite the opposite—now he is adding an extra, novel, and radically impossible kind of righteousness of works, founded on the stubborn vanity of the way chosen by man in rebellion. When God says of his law, Do this and live, see now if you can earn salvation, man is not being shown again the kind of ability and power he was given in integrity and which he may think he now has but has lost. Rather, he is being shown the impossibility of the notion of ability he attempted to arrogate to himself in sin, which actually he never had nor was supposed to have. The legal promise does not reflect the established, normal, covenantal relation of man's creation; rather, it reflects the fugitive, vain, abnormal dream of man in sin.

All this profoundly colors the handling of law in the Reformed church. With the transvaluation made by the Westminster Confession, there is a certain inherent and universal constitutionality to the righteousness of works in the Old Testament. In law and legal promise there is revealed that which is instituted in the framework of the cosmos and the charter of God's dealings with the human race. A cast of legalism overshadows all theology. When before federalism Calvin found for law a place eternal and

basic to the ways of God, he could do so without the corresponding legalism. Law as a pattern for the life of gratitude belongs in
the scheme of things. It has a proper use. But the legal promises
wrung from God are neither basic nor eternal; they are a mode
of working which God has adopted as a temporary expedient, a
divine reckoning with and accommodation to the illusions of
man. In the fullness of the knowledge of grace, Calvin is able to
set aside legalism in a way that later Reformed theology, committed to the law of works in perpetual validity, is wholly unable
to do.

3. The Law of Nature and the Order of Grace

So much for law in Judaism. There is a corresponding law
among the Gentiles. The law of the covenant is echoed in the law
of nature. The original order of nature, reversed though it is in
sin, yet remains in residue. The obliterated image of God sur-
vives as a relic. Natural man is blinded; yet within his darkness,
some sparks of truth flash forth. We turn now to Calvin's account
of the moral sense.

The grace of God surmounts the obstacle of sin and, though it
does not regenerate and purify, founds an ethic which orders the
societies of men and preserves man within the sphere of his concupiscence. The law given to the Gentiles is extensively treated in
Calvin's Commentary on Romans.

> They by their deeds declare themselves to have some rule of
> righteousness, for there is no people so lost to humanity that they
> do not keep themselves within some laws. Since therefore all
> people voluntarily and with no teacher are inclined to make laws
> for themselves, it is established beyond question that there are
> naturally engrafted in the minds of men certain conceptions of
> justice and rectitude, which the Greeks call προλήψεις, and
> which are implanted by nature in the hearts of men. They there-
> fore have a law, without the law; for although they do not have
> the written law of Moses, they are by no means completely lacking
> in the knowledge of right and justice.[17]

Calvin is willing to grant such virtue all manner of likeness or similitude to true virtue but will never grant it any substantial reality.
His carefully chosen vocabulary is significant. It is not virtue, but
the *external resemblance* of virtue, the *lifeless image* of the right,

not righteousness but *counterfeit* righteousness. "There is a likeness [*conformité*] between the law of God and the order of nature which is engraven in all men."[18] An analogical likeness exists between real and counterfeit virtue, yet there is no identity—as an image may resemble but is not composed of the original reality, or a shadow in darkness conforms to the outline of a lighted object. The divine distinction between the just and the unjust shines through the veil of sin and creates an ethical fabric woven on a relative scale within the natural and sinful world. Real virtue casts its shadow, though it does not itself appear.

The natural man is obligated to this law, as it images true morality. Though successful performance is "of no avail to justification," it is blessed by God so far as it is morally correct and objectively parallel to true righteousness.

> God is sometimes said to love those whom he does not approve or justify; for, since the preservation of the human race is agreeable to Him—which consists in justice, uprightness, moderation, prudence, fidelity, and temperance—he is said to love the political virtues; not that they are meritorious of salvation or of grace, but that they have reference to an end of which he approves. In this sense, under various points of view, God loved Aristides and Fabricius, and also hated them . . . he loved his own work in them; but as their heart was impure, the outward semblance of righteousness was of no avail for obtaining righteousness.[19]

Readers often find Calvin's account irritating in its oscillation between praise of the philosophic virtues and denigration of them. It will sometimes seem as if Calvin fails to preserve any useful distinction between natural virtues and authentic ones.

Basically though, very clearly in certain passages, Calvin sets these works aside because they are inevitably and invariably done in self-trust and not in response to the grace of God. All natural obedience is tinged with legalism and self-merit which makes it different not just in degree but in kind. Whether or not Calvin's analysis is true to modern assessments of religious phenomena is an issue we must forgo, but his account is revelatory of his presuppositions. The question of natural ethical value is to be dealt with not only at the level of moral law, but also and more fundamentally in the light of divine grace. The difference between counterfeit and real virtue is *internal,* or attitudinal.

When we remember that the end of what is right is always to serve God, whatever is directed to any other end, can have no claim to that appellation. Therefore, since they regard not the end prescribed by Divine wisdom, though an act performed by them be externally and apparently good, yet, being directed to a wrong end, it becomes sin.[20]

"Man seeks himself in everything, even in God," wrote Luther wistfully, and Calvin concurs.

The natural virtues are concupiscent. The noblest of the philosophers are in the condition of Paul, Pharisee of the Pharisees, who kept the law but overlooked the sinfulness of the autonomous self-will. Concupiscence, we recall, is one of Calvin's categories for understanding the primal sin. But the natural man never dreams that this, which generates all his virtues, is his chief sin. The philosophers permitted it; so did Paul also, until he found it rather the source of his sin. His affections were so concupiscently disordered as to make him, for all his outward righteousness, the chief of sinners, since "being puffed up with confidence in his righteousness, he expected salvation by his works."[21] The natural man is caught unawares, as was Paul, in concupiscent self-will, which discolors all his virtues.

> In the universal observation of the law, the censure of concupiscence wholly escapes our notice. For the natural man cannot be brought to acknowledge the disorders of his inward affections. The light of nature is smothered, before it approaches the first entrance of this abyss.[22]
>
> Our judgment does indeed agree with the law of God in regard to the mere outward actions; but concupiscence, which is the source of everything evil, escapes our notice.[23]

Like a minus sign before an algebraic parenthesis, man's presuming effort to provide works for his salvation inverts and reverses everything. Presently we see how federal theology obscured and even reversed Calvin here, for in the universal covenant of works man is asked to provide just such works, and his sin is his failure so to do. But in Calvin, virtuous natural man is guilty fundamentally because he trusts in his own work and not in God. Even as they professed to serve God, Aristides and the Greeks of legendary virtue actually trusted in themselves.

> *Trust* in God . . . is the mother of piety. We recognize that some persons have been so highly endowed with integrity as to have obtained among men the praise of being perfectly just. . . . But even with all the excellence of their virtues, those men were either filled with ambition, or inflated with pride, which made them *trust* more in themselves than in God. . . . Relying on their own strength of virtue, such persons despised the grace of God with all the arrogance of impiety. Idolizing their own virtue, they disdained to lift up their eyes to him.[24]

Salvation by works is characteristic in some form of every natural religion, and the effort to do this involves man's spurning God's grace and assuming rights that are not his. The Sermons on Ephesians, chapter 1, make this claim (the accuracy of which we cannot investigate) with particular clarity.

> If a man asks the philosophers, they will always say that God loves those that are worthy, that because virtue pleases him he selects those who devote themselves to it and preserves them for his people. . . . Bringing their own free will, the pagans thought themselves bound to God for nothing except their own good fortune, as they called it, for they believed that they had everything through their own virtue [*vertu,* strength] and industry.[25]

The question is where they put their trust, and its answer reveals the ultimate sin of self-trust thwarting the grace of God. When judged not so much because of laws broken as for grace spurned, even in his virtue man moves away from God to self-dependence, and so stands totally depraved. The more the philosophers thought themselves approaching God, the further from him they fell.

> Men of this class will with astonishing security trust in themselves . . . [and] are commonly transported with prosperity, as though they had merited the Lord's kindness by their good deeds . . . And though all the gifts of God are so many evidences of his paternal goodness, yet as he often has a different object in view, the ungodly absurdly congratulate themselves on their prosperity, as though they were dear to him, while he kindly and bountifully supports them. . . . the Lord by his kindness shows to us, that it is he to whom we ought to turn, if we desire to secure our wellbeing, and at the same time he strengthens our confidence in expecting mercy. If we use not God's bounty for this end, we abuse it. . . . it will then be found, that it will be justly imputed to them as an extreme wickedness, that they had been made worse through God's bounty, by which they ought surely to have been improved.[26]

All philosophic virtues, as they call them, which men think they possess through free-will, are mere fumes; nay, they are the delusions of the devil, by which he bewitches the minds of men, so that they come not to God, but, on the contrary, precipitate themselves into the lowest depth, where they seek to exalt themselves beyond measure.[27]

4. The Law of Nature and the Covenant of Works

The theology enshrined in the Westminster standards speaks with as much or more conviction than did Calvin of the divine law written on the heart of the natural man. As was true with its account of law in Judaism, there is a certain similarity to that concept of natural law which Calvin had bequeathed his church; but there are underlying differences which ought not be obscured. What the light of nature provides is a more or less accurate statement to the natural man of the covenant of works. The earliest rise of federal theology involves a combining of the Mosaic covenant with a primitive and general *lex naturae.* A partial or total identification of the two becomes a fundamental argument of all writers. The legal covenant of Moses is made a general covenant, founded by God with man at creation. The specific restatement of the covenant of works at Sinai has a universal parallel in a recurring statement of it in the conscience of man. One of the older terms for what came to be best known as the covenant of works is the *foedus naturae,* the covenant of nature.

So the light of nature with which the Westminster Confession begins teaches man law and thereby informs him of God's original and universal terms of life. Calvin had found widespread in the minds of men the notion that man ought to strive by his own will and strength to merit salvation in obedience to law. But that which was for Calvin an illusion of sin is now ascribed rather to the voice of God speaking to man through his reason and urging him to that righteousness of works for which he was created. Fisher and Turretin will suffice to make this claim explicit:

It is . . . the general opinion of men's reason throughout the whole world, that righteousness is gotten by the works of the law; and the reason is, because the covenant was engendered in the minds of men in the very creation, so that man naturally can judge no otherwise of the law than as of a covenant of works, which was given to make righteous, and to give life and salvation. . . .

> As all men are born under the covenant of works, they are nat-
> urally prone to conceive that the favour of God, and all good things,
> do depend and follow upon their obedience to the law, and that the
> wrath of God, and all evil things, do depend and follow their dis-
> obedience to it.[28]

> As the former [covenant] was made in the state of nature, so it was
> known by nature, and impressed upon the consciences of men, in
> which the work of the law was written.[29]

Shifting presuppositions have once again removed Reformed
theology far from Calvin's account, this time in its apologetic
judgment of the natural man. We must now say that man through
reason does have, basically and correctly, at least in form, a vision
of the life for which he was created. To this extent, he knows God,
the god of the general and natural covenant. He has the law; all
he lacks is the ability to keep it. Reformed theology was not so
naïve, of course, as to suppose that man apart from revelation
had the law in all particulars. His sin was more complicated than
that. The giving again of the law at Sinai was necessitated by
the fact that the law had become much encrusted with error. This
is part of man's sinfulness; he ignores and forgets the law. But it is
fundamental to Reformed apologetics that if man is thoughtful
and alert even in the state of nature, he knows more or less correctly the ways of God in dealing with the race of men, at least
in these important areas of duty, sin, and judgment. None of this
knowledge is of avail anymore to salvation, but man can and does
correctly estimate the terms, if not the details, of the God-man
contract, so far as the universal relation of God with man is concerned. That God's course is different with the elect in the covenant of grace, and that the Westminster divines give God's other
course exhaustive attention, does not alter the essential correctness
of man's natural acquaintance with God. With this as a basis of
apologetics, Reformed thought subsequently gave increased emphasis to the place of the conscience, supplementing it where necessary with the law of Sinai, and judged the natural man so far as
his sin was a want of conformity unto or a transgression of the law
of God. We shall return to this when we deal with man's culpability, in chapter 7.

From Calvin's viewpoint, far from being a correct recollection of the original terms of salvation, this natural way of works is rather the product of human arrogance. In nature God's invitation is to confidence and trust in divine goodness. But man prefers self-trust. The Gentile world, like the Jewish, dreams of a righteousness of works. So God lets law be for them too a kind of divine righteousness, wherein he makes a certain condescension to their stubbornness in sin. "The Gentiles have naturally the righteousness of the law engraven on their minds . . ."[30] But this does not mean that it reflects man's original kind of righteousness, any more than does the legal, Mosaic promise. On the contrary, just as the legal promise is more the fugitive presumption of man in sin than it is the foundational principle of God, so the naturally engraven righteousness of the law is God's way of reaching through to man in sin despite his conceit and self-will. Men ought to obey this law. But their sense of obligation is so perverted that their attitude in keeping it is more a product of their sin than of God's invitation and authorization. When man is blinded to God's fatherly invitation to trust in him, God then uses natural law to invite the stubborn sinner to trust in himself. This orders society, and produces a certain counterfeit righteousness, relics of authentic virtues. But it does not lead to trust, and therefore it does not save, for this righteousness of works in the natural man is a distorted plan of salvation unmistakably more of man's making than of God's.

In the Westminster standards, the sin of man in nature is his disobedience to the law of works, while in the thought of Calvin, though it is true that sin is disobedience to natural law, more fundamentally sin is man's self-willed obedience to it. At Westminster, we can condemn works under the natural and Mosaic law only because they are not sufficient to meet the rigorous demands of the covenant of works. We are no longer able to measure these deeds by whether in them man is motivated by the attempt to raise himself up apart from the Lord or by a grateful dependence on divine grace.

CHAPTER 5
The Righteousness of God

The pivotal figures in Christian thought have found, often as not, that what troubled them most was the "righteousness of God," and that light broke over their agonizing search with a re-understanding of that concept. This was certainly Paul's experience; and when Luther underwent the same struggle, the Reformation was born of his new grasp of the *iustitia Dei*. Like his German counterpart, the Geneva Reformer worked his way out of medieval Catholicism to an eminently Protestant and Christian understanding of God's righteousness. But the insights of the first generation of Reformers were not to survive; they were eclipsed in the century following, and had been wholly lost by the time we reached the Westminster Confession. To Calvin's recovery of the biblical concept of God's righteousness, and the subsequent inability of Reformed thinkers to retain it, we now turn.

1. The Righteousness of God and the Mercy of God

The following remarkable definition of the righteousness of God occurs in Calvin's *Institutes*, a statement the more revealing as it is at once outside the context of systematic treatment of divine attributes and yet the only definition of God's righteousness in the *Institutes*.

> [God] announces in what character he will be known by us . . . These three things it is certainly of the highest importance for us to know—*mercy*, in which alone consists all our salvation; *judgment*, which is executed on the wicked every day, and awaits them in a still heavier degree to eternal destruction; *righteousness, by which the faithful are preserved, and most graciously supported.*[1]

How is it that Calvin thinks of righteousness in God as graciously preserving and supporting, so that righteousness is allied with mercy and somewhat an opposite of judgment? Characteristically in Reformed theology as set forth in the Westminster Confession, has it not been the other way round? God's righteousness has been synonymous with judgment and often quite the opposite of mercy.

Calvin supports this definition with an appeal to Jeremiah 9. In the Commentary on Jeremiah he is quite clear that the common notion (and the one to which the Westminster standards return) is a misconception.

> God's righteousness is not to be taken according to what is commonly understood by it. They speak incorrectly who represent God's righteousness as in opposition to his mercy. Hence comes the common saying, "I appeal from righteousness [justice] to mercy." The Scripture speaks differently. By *righteousness* is meant that faithful protection of God with which he defends and preserves his own people; by *judgment* is meant the rigor which he exercises against the transgressors of the law. . . . When God declares that he does righteousness, he gives us a reason for confidence; he thus promises to be the guardian of our salvation. For, as I have said, his righteousness is not to render to everyone his just reward, but is to be extended further and is to be taken for his faithfulness. . . . His righteousness is such that he will never leave us destitute of help when necessary.[2]

God's righteousness is that in his nature which demands a return to the government he instituted for man. It therefore has a twofold office. It is set irrevocably against sin. There is in Calvin a full place for the prosecuting of iniquity by the divine righteousness. We come afterward to this. But we first have to remember the character of this original order, to which God presses as he judges the world in righteousness. Ideally, God was gracious to man and man grateful to God; this was man's primal rectitude. Consequently God is also and fundamentally righteous as he pours out his righteousness for man. Judgment and mercy are both inseparably allied with righteousness, and both flow from it.

God *rectifies* his order. "It is the glory of our faith that God, the Creator of the world, does not disregard or abandon the order which he himself at first established."[3] His demand for its restoration issues in a condemnation of man and his sin; but this demand is simultaneously for a return to an order of grace, and from this it is by his righteousness that God redeems man and is gracious. Accordingly, there is in Calvin an extended series of passages, notably in his lectures on Psalms and the prophets, which later Reformed thought was systemically incompetent to understand, where Calvin sets forth the divine righteousness as part of the vocabulary of salvation, quite in keeping with the brief definition of the *Institutes.* We quote at length sufficient to establish this point beyond all doubt.

> By *the righteousness [iustitia] of God,* which he [the Psalmist] engages to celebrate, we are to understand his goodness; for this attribute, as usually applied to God in the Scriptures, does not so much denote the strictness with which he exacts vengeance, as his faithfulness in fulfilling the promises and extending help to all who seek him in the hour of need.[4]

> I have often before had occasion to observe, that *the righteousness of God* does not mean that property of his nature by which he renders to every man his own, but the faithfulness which he observes towards his own people, when he cherishes, defends, and delivers them. Hence the inestimable consolation which arises from learning that our salvation is so inseparably linked with the righteousness of God, as to have the same stability with this Divine attribute. . . . The Psalmist connects this salvation with righteousness, as the effect with the cause; for his confident persuasion of obtaining salvation proceeded solely from reflecting that God is righteous [just], and that he cannot deny himself.[5]

> Salvation . . . is, properly speaking, the effect of righteousness. . . . I may add, that the righteousness of God, which is the source of salvation, does not consist in his recompensing men according to their works, but is just the illustration of his mercy, grace, and faithfulness.[6]

> To *goodness* is subjoined *righteousness,* a word, as we have had occasion frequently to observe before, denoting the protection by which God defends and preserves his own people. He is then called righteous, not because he rewards every man according to his desert, but because he deals faithfully with his saints, in spreading the hand of his protection over them.[7]

> By God's righteousness we should understand, as before remarked, his goodness toward those who trust him. It does not mean what impious men foolishly imagine: that God rewards works with salvation. They catch the word "righteousness" and suppose that the freely given blessings of God come rather on account of our merits.

But God shows his righteousness in quite another way, and so
speaks differently. In order to show how dear and precious our
salvation is to him, God does indeed say that he plans to give proof
of his righteousness in delivering us. But the meaning of this word
"righteousness" includes something more. God has promised that
our salvation will be his concern; hence he reveals himself as righteous whenever he delivers us from our troubles. So the righteousness of God ought not to be referred to the merit of works, but
rather to the promise by which he has bound himself to us. In a
similar sense God is often called faithful. In short, the righteousness
and faithfulness of God mean the same thing.[8]

The New Testament confirms this, as God's righteousness
engages to give what it requires. To distributive righteousness,
there is added communicative righteousness. It can be said, of
course, that grace gives what righteousness asks. But it is equally
proper to say that righteousness gives what righteousness asks.
This passage from the *Institutes* shows Calvin's incorporation of
his exegesis into his systematic theology. Our justification is a function of divine justice. Righteousness in God is offensive, fighting
for man, not less than defensive, pressing against man.

We see how frequently and earnestly the Scripture urges us to give
praise to God alone whenever righteousness [*iustitia*] is concerned.
The apostle even assures us that the Lord's design in conferring
righteousness upon us in Christ is to demonstrate his own righteousness (Rom. 3:25). Immediately he adds the nature of this
showing of his righteousness: it is that he might be recognized as
righteous [*iust*] and the one who justifies [*iustifico,* make righ-
teous] him who has faith in Jesus Christ. God's righteousness, we
see, is not sufficiently illustrated unless he alone is esteemed righteous and unless he communicates the grace of righteousness
[*iustitia gratia*] to the undeserving. . . .

Let us remember, therefore, in the whole discussion concerning
righteousness, to keep this end in view: that all the praise of righteousness may remain perfect and undiminished with the Lord,
since, according to the apostle's testimony, he has bestowed his
grace upon us in order to demonstrate his own righteousness.[9]

It is of this new, fuller revealing of God's righteousness apart
from law that Paul speaks in Romans 1 and 3. "Righteousness of
God" has to do with the status of man; a righteousness with God,
"that which is approved at his tribunal." But, insists Calvin, the

expression has to do initially with the divine perfection, God's righteousness, which communicates itself to man and makes him righteous. The righteousness which God confers has its ground in the righteous character of God. The many prophetic passages about this activity of divine righteousness are the antecedents to Paul's thought, notes Calvin. Law also, but differently, bears witness to it, showing that righteousness cannot come from man, but must come from God's self-impartation. Calvin writes in the Commentary on Romans:

> God's righteousness was clearly revealed only when Christ appeared. This is a definition of that righteousness . . . made known in the gospel. He [Paul] affirms that it consists of two parts: The first is that God is righteous, not indeed as one among many, but as the one who contains in himself alone all the fullness of righteousness. He receives the full and complete praise which is his due only as he alone obtains the name and honor of being righteous. . . .
>
> The other part refers to the *communication of righteousness,* for God certainly does not shut up his riches within himself, but pours them forth upon mankind. God's righteousness, therefore, shines in us insofar as he makes us righteous by faith in Christ.[10]

Both this statement and that from the *Institutes* show that God's righteousness is not fully known unless it is known as a *communicative righteousness,* as well as a *distributive righteousness,* a righteousness to be shared as well as preserved.

At the beginning, man was established to live by his participation in divine righteousness. Rather than living through his own self-righteousness, he was to receive righteousness from God. So when righteousness is gifted again in the gospel, the primal order is but re-established. Calvin conceives of these two participation processes as being somewhat different. That there are now offenses to be canceled and that the justified man remains still a sinner in part means that imputation is involved, whereas in Adam, as integral man, there was but impartation. But imputed and imparted righteousness are in thrust the same, in that never is righteousness of human authorship; it always rests in, flows from, and is borrowed from God, the source of righteousness.

> God alone is the fountain of righteousness, and we are righteous only by a participation in him, yet . . . we have been alienated

from his righteousness through the unhappy breach occasioned by the fall . . .[11]

Here we are shown what is the source of all evils: that is, our withdrawing from him who is the fountain of all righteousness.[12]

Man's sin is not so much that he brought God no inherent righteousness of his own, but that "Adam departed from the fountain of righteousness."[13]

The law does condemn man because he has no righteousness of his own. In his sin man shuts off the divine fountain of righteousness, and then God through law casts man into an economy of man's own fabrication. Then righteousness in God which originally and ideally designs both to give and to require can but require. God cannot pour out his righteousness, but through it in law he yet demands. When man proposes to manufacture a righteousness satisfactory to God, he is soon shut up in his own legal, impossible way of self-righteousness. It is the dispensation of law to show this distributive face of the divine righteousness. But when law has done its pedagogical and psychological work, it is set aside, and God re-establishes his original righteousness, communicating it in the gospel.

2. The Righteousness of God and the Judgment of God

Such righteousness can only be an unqualified *no* toward the life which man has chosen. Condemnation is the reciprocal of redemption, but without tension. Equally significant with the fact that God wills a return to grace is the fact that this is no compromise affair, but an unqualified return to the kind of rectitude for which we were created. So Calvin is fully at home with God's judging the world in righteousness.

God knows how to bring all things into order and into a state of perfection, for it is said that at the coming of our Lord Jesus Christ, when he shall appear to judge the world, there will be a restoration of all things.[14]

The work of God is to judge the world, that is, to *rectify* it by his righteousness, and reduce to the best order any disorder which may be in it. . . . He is by nature judge; he must of necessity be righteous, for he cannot deny himself.[15]

> Our present disorder, ἀταξία, is a sign of the judgment which does not yet appear. For if God is the righteous judge of the world, the present confusion must of necessity be restored to order.[16]

Righteousness is therefore a reaction in God against sin. It is something self-respecting in God which is offended and has to be vindicated. If asked the question, why must sin be punished, Calvin's answer is, because God is righteous. When Calvin warns in the *Institutes,* the Commentary on Psalms, the Commentary on Jeremiah, and elsewhere that righteousness means more than a distribution of just deserts, he does not mean to deny that this too is its function. God's righteousness requires a certain satisfaction. It searches for righteousness in man, and where it finds none, it condemns. Judgment follows the violation of God's righteousness.

> We hold it as a settled principle that the nature of God is righteous and that it is no more possible for him to turn aside from right and equity than it is for him to say that he will renounce his being and no longer be God. . . . God must hate us. We know that he is the fountain of all righteousness and that there is no agreement between him and iniquity.[17]

Law demonstrates this. To the man who dreams that he has some righteousness of his own, there is given the law as a perfect rule of divine righteousness. Law in grace, not law alone, was and is God's pattern for righteousness in man. But law alone, the legal promise, remains when man falls into the way of self-righteousness. Technically, strictly, as we saw in the preceding chapter, this is an impossible righteousness. Yet God condescends to establish a righteousness of works.

When Calvin teaches then that law reveals the righteousness of God, he means that law alone shows us all that righteousness *demands.* He does not mean that law alone shows us all that God's righteousness *does,* for have we not just seen at length that there is a fuller righteousness, apart from the law? But God makes a "first preparation" for the re-establishing of his righteousness by setting before us his law. In demanding from us a righteousness of our own, he desires to force us to abandon our own, and be opened up to embrace that righteousness which he communicates. Calvin so arranges the sequence of paragraphs in the *Instruction in Faith*.

> In the Law of God a perfect standard of all righteousness is presented to us which with good reason can be called the eternal will of the Lord. . . .

> Behold above, therefore, the standard of a just and holy life and even a very perfect image of justice or righteousness, so that if someone expresses the Law of God in his life, he will lack nothing of the perfection required before the Lord.

> . . . the Law . . . becomes . . . an occasion of sin and death. For, since we are all convicted of being transgressors of the Law, the more clearly the Law discloses to us the justice of God, the more it uncovers on the other hand our iniquity.[18]

From this viewpoint, there is a contrast between law and gospel, righteousness and grace. The contrast is made under the assumption that righteousness ought to be something of human authorship; it is made by men who are appreciative only of that in the righteousness of God which requires, and who are oblivious of the giving, gospel righteousness. It is a contrast restricted to the legal, pedagogical dispensation, limited to the sinful mind. It disappears where righteousness is fully known. But it is a valid contrast. This passage from the *Instruction in Faith*, repeated in the *Institutes*, is representative:

> For, in the Law he [God] appeared only as remunerator of perfect righteousness (of which we are completely destitute) and, on the other hand, as upright and severe judge of sins. But in Christ his face shines full of grace and kindliness even toward miserable and unworthy sinners . . .[19]

Significantly and more frequently, however, Calvin prefers the contrast of mercy with judgment. This is more natural to him, for the single activity of the divine righteousness has the double and opposite outcome, mercy and judgment.

> God's mercy alone is that which delivers us from the dread and terror of judgment. . . . the judgment of condemnation is suspended over the whole world, and nothing but mercy can bring relief. . . . mercy itself in a manner triumphs, and alone reigns when the severity of judgment gives way; . . . the faithful know that the wrath of God in a manner yields to mercy . . .[20]

Even judgment, notes Calvin, is properly a cause for hope, not fear, when it is known in its wider reference of rectifying the original order.[21] And the contrast between God's righteousness and his mercy, however proper to theological apologetics, is partial and has its resolution in the inseparable alliance between God's righteousness and his grace.

3. Grace, Righteousness, and the Covenants

The proponents of the theology of the Westminster Confession see Calvin with a new set of spectacles, the paired covenants. What they see is a remarkable commentary on the influence of our presuppositions as we read the work of another. With alarming velocity and ferocity, grace and righteousness are set as opposites in a way far removed from the intention and use of Calvin. There is grist for their mill in Calvin, as we have just seen; but what is for Calvin a half-truth becomes for the Calvinists the substructure of their classical creed. Never in all Christian thought has the contrariety between righteousness and grace been so sharply drawn as in Reformed theology of the seventeenth and eighteenth centuries. The contrast, which had preceded in scholastic usage, and from which Luther and Calvin had escaped at the cost of a Reformation, now returns with a double vengeance. The dialectic of covenants that underlies all systematizing of theology has for its tectonic theme a polarity and confrontation of righteousness with grace.

> There are only two general covenants, the legal, and the evangelical. . . . The first in order is the legal covenant of works. It is founded upon the attribute of *justice*. Its promise is, "Do this and thou shalt live." This covenant failed upon the part of man, in the fall of Adam. The second is the evangelical covenant, founded upon the attribute of *mercy*.[22]

> This double covenant is proposed to us in Scriptures: of nature and of faith. . . . The former rests upon a just Creator, the latter upon a merciful Redeemer.[23]

> The one was carried out in the *court of righteousness* [*iustitia*], in which either a sentence of acquittal was pronounced upon the just, or of condemnation upon the sinner, because there was no hope of pardon; the other in the *court of mercy,* where a sentence of absolution is pronounced upon sinners, but believing and penitent. . . .

The object of the first was the declaration of the righteousness, but of the second the manifestation of the mercy and exceeding love of God. In that, the strict severity of the lawgiver and judge played its part, by which there was no room for repentance, so neither for pardon. But in this, the forbearance of the Father appears, who opened the way to grace and salvation of the sinner.[24]

So far as the universal covenant applies, by which God judges all but the elect, righteousness in God issues absolute claims, then searches the works of man for something deserving and satisfactory. How different from that of Calvin in his *Institutes* has the Genevan definition of righteousness become by the time we reach Turretin and his *Institutes!*

These [several attributes of God] however can be referred to two principal ones, which embrace the others under them, righteousness [*iustitia*] and goodness. The former is that by which God is in himself holy and just, and has the constant will of giving each his due. The latter is that by which he is conceived as the supreme good, and giver of all good.[25]

The covenant writers are not unaware that Scripture sometimes uses *iustitia* in a broader sense. Turretin makes place for a *iustitia universalis* which embraces the "universal complex of all virtues," and to which his benignity, beneficence, and constancy belong. But his covenantal presuppositions are such that he cannot take this as anything other than a figurative speaking. All his concern is with the *iustitia particularis,* the proper righteousness of God "which gives to each his due," is occupied with the distribution of rewards and punishments, and is called *distributive,* having a "going out" (*egressus*) and activity essential to God in his *iustitia vindicatrix.*[26]

There is not the slightest hint in the Westminster Confession that righteousness in God is anything more than a demanding attribute which rigidly compensates and therefore inevitably condemns. Following a reference to his "most righteous will" and "most just and terrible" judgments in the definition of God, the Confession next invokes the justice (righteousness) of God in connection with those excluded from the covenant of grace. "The rest of mankind, God was pleased . . . to pass by, and to ordain them to dishonour and wrath for their sin, to the praise of his

glorious justice."[27] The frequent references to righteousness thereafter portray it as sovereign, mysterious, impartial, aloof. The concluding chapter expects a final judgment in which mercy will
save and righteousness damn.

> God hath appointed a day, wherein he will judge the world in righ-
> teousness by Jesus Christ. . . . The end of God's appointing this day,
> is for the manifestation of the glory of his mercy in the eternal sal-
> vation of the elect; and of his justice in the damnation of the rep-
> robate, who are wicked and disobedient.[28]

The increasing use of the English *justice,* which as well as *righteousness* translates the Latin *iustitia,* is significant. The Confession simply does not know the larger righteousness of God.
God's righteousness seeks to bring man to justice; it does not
seek to bring righteousness to man. It is to be feared and escaped,
hardly celebrated and cherished.

Originally and universally still, God lays down the terms of
the covenant of justice, whereupon it is left to man to "attain to
righteousness" (Larger Catechism).[29] Following a disclaimer that
righteousness is never intrinsic but always *ex pacto,* Turretin goes
on to make this comparison of the covenants:

> This [first covenant] demanded antecedently a proper and personal
> obedience, by which man both obtained his own justification
> [*iustificatio*] before God, and life as the stipulated reward of his
> labors.[30]

> The former consisted in man's giving a perfect righteousness; the
> latter in his receiving the infinite righteousness of God.[31]

Original righteousness is not received; it is achieved. God does not
endow man with it; man produces it for God. Man's iniquity is
his default in creditable attainment, and not, as it was for Calvin,
a departure from the divine fountain of righteousness.

This results in a kind of chronic stress in God. In the natural
covenant men universally have merited God's wrath; in the evangelical covenant some men particularly receive his love, when
God's sympathy gets the better of his severity. The following passage from Fisher is representative of the schizophrenic God so
portrayed:

> For *Truth* and *Justice* stood up and said, that man had sinned, and
> therefore man must die; and so called for the condemnation of a

sinful, and therefore worthily a cursed creature; or else they must be violated: for thou saidst, (said they to God,) "In that day that thou eatest of the tree of knowledge of good and evil, thou shalt die the death." *Mercy,* on the other side, pleaded for favour, and appeals to the great court in heaven: and there it pleads, saying, Wisdom, and power, and goodness, have been all manifest in the creation; and anger and justice have been magnified in man's misery that he is now plunged into by his fall: but I have not yet been manifested. O let favour and compassion be shown towards man, wofully seduced and overthrown by Satan! Oh! said they unto God, it is a royal thing to relieve the distressed; and the greater any one is, the more placable and gentle he ought to be. But *Justice* replied, If I be offended, I must be satisfied and have my right; and therefore I require, that man, who hath lost himself by his disobedience, should, for remedy, set obedience against it, and so satisfy the judgment of God. Therefore the wisdom of God became an umpire, and devised a way to reconcile them; concluding, that before there could be reconciliation made, there must be . . . a satisfaction of God's justice.[82]

The umpire's decision reveals that the alliance of truth with justice is not coincidental!

The understanding of the atonement reflects at its core this dilemma between justice and mercy. This precedence of justice and its demands makes federal thought a receptive climate for penal satisfactory theories of the atonement, for in this *opus operatum* God's inner conflicts are resolved. This is the work of all works. Christ, notes the Westminster Confession, "was made under the law," both perfectly fulfilling it and enduring its torments, and so "hath fully satisfied the justice of his Father."[33] The supposition is that the normative covenant had to be satisfied by this better Adam before the covenant of mercy could be instituted, or consummated. Fisher makes this supposition explicit:

And thus did our Lord Jesus Christ enter into the same covenant of works that Adam did to deliver believers from it: he was contented to be under all that commanding, revenging authority, which that covenant had over them, to free them from the penalty of it . . .[34]

A. A. Hodge writes in his *Commentary on the Confession of Faith:*

The essential justice of the divine nature demands the punishment of sin. It demands also that the condition of the original covenant of works should be fulfilled before the reward is granted. The latter, Christ does by his obedience. The former, he suffers in the sorrows of his life and death.[35]

None noticed the damage done to the person of Jesus in relation to his Father by foisting on him a bifurcated life lived simultaneously under law and under grace, proving the mercy of God by enduring his justice.

Calvin may draw this contrast between mercy and righteousness, though it is surprisingly absent from his writings. And he knows of a way that God's justice must be satisfied. But he can assert these things without distortion. It is minimally with him an equilibrium, never a tension, because he does not operate with an underlying covenant of justice at variance with a covenant of mercy. And he knows well the complementary emphasis that exalts righteousness as one of God's saving perfections.

Meanwhile, to the narrowed vision of the Westminster divines, the gospel reveals nothing further about the righteousness of God, for that is fully seen in the law. What it does further reveal is a substitute righteousness which God's mercy has procured, and which is quite other than the righteousness normally demanded. The "righteousness of God" that Paul proclaims in Romans is now understood as a technical term, idiomatic for a contrived righteousness which contrasts strongly with the generally required righteousness of works, and which for believers is now recognized in lieu of it. It does not flow from, but rather, by tour de force, circumvents and placates righteousness in God. It shields the believer from divine righteousness. It is not that righteousness in God now, apart from law, conveys itself to man, but rather that "rich grace" has gone beyond and "purchased" an escape from the "exact justice" of God, Christ having made "a proper, real, and full satisfaction to his Father's justice," thereby to "discharge" it and "procure his favor."[36] A reading of the Confession's chapter "Of Justification" will show how thoroughly it has excluded Calvin's insistent claim that righteousness in God is communicative as well as vindicatory. The righteousness of Romans is an improvised righteousness that is the product of God's mercy having overcome his justice. Many notable Reformed commentators on Romans, such as Hodge or Shedd, who otherwise read Calvin

closely, overlook entirely in Calvin's Commentary on Romans the
presence of a communicable righteousness, because their presuppositions about righteousness are so restricted.

The great systematist of the Swiss Reformation, like the
prophet of that in Germany, perceived that when God in Christ
invests the man of faith with righteousness, he is not doing something radically different and wholly out of keeping with what was
first instituted for man. He is only doing what he set out to do
at the start: to be a fountain of righteousness to man. This involves no inconsistency. There is no tension, such as that proposed by the Calvinists who would have God's attribute of righteousness, the foundation of the first covenant, insist on its own
way, then, satisfaction having been provided, step into the background; to be followed by his attribute of mercy, providing for
man a novel righteousness, which righteousness in God can per-
mit but for which it could never have provided. For Calvin,
rather, when man now lives by a righteousness that is not his
own but God's for him, God is being the same God who drew
Adam into righteousness.

The righteousness of God that only demands is not the character of God in himself, but the character that sin has given God.
In the legal promise God appears as he must to drive us out of
the impossible way of self-justification we have chosen. He shows
us neither what we are capable of nor what we were created for;
he shows us our delusion. When that illusion is burst, then we see
the full character of righteousness in God, and exalt with Calvin
the divine "righteousness, by which the faithful are preserved and
most graciously supported." No theology which fails to rejoice
in the saving righteousness of God ought to be called authenti-
cally Reformed, for it has lost one of the richest insights of the
Reformation.

CHAPTER 6

Responsible Man:
His Accountability

We have largely avoided the word "responsibility" in preceding chapters, although the path we have traveled has circumscribed that complex area of man's life under God of which the center is responsibility. Grace, works, duty, sin, law, righteousness —all the concepts invoked are tangents to an understanding of responsibility. And these concepts appear on almost every page that Calvin wrote. By contrast, *responsibility* (in Latin or French equivalents) does not occur in Calvin, nor in the Westminster Confession or the earlier covenant writers. *Responsible* in its present usage has developed since. Neither is it a word found in the Bible. All use simpler language. But we are now in a position to press the question of responsibility, integrating the component concepts into a comprehensive reply.

We have already spoken of the duty of man in terms of his *response* and *acknowledgment*. Such language in Calvin reorients the focus of responsibility. For modern man, to speak of man's responsibility lays emphasis on the initiative and activity of man. In Calvin though, where this is a *response-ability,* there is always the double emphasis on both God and man. Initiative is first and principally with God; man responds to what God has done. We can profitably bring this to focus now in terms of man's obligation and accountability.

1. Man's Obligation

Calvin uses the concept of *obligation* (etymologically the same in French and Latin), and many related words with the root idea of binding. *Religion* has also, and not incidentally, this

root. Man's *natural obligation,* or his true *religion,* prefaces an
exposition of the Ten Commandments; we here learn

> . . . that God, as he is our Creator, justly sustains towards us the
> character of a Father and of a Lord; and that on this account we
> *owe* to him glory and reverence, love and fear. Moreover, [we
> learn] that we are not at liberty to follow every thing to which the
> violence of our passions may incite us; but that we *ought* to be atten-
> tive to his will, and to practise nothing but what is pleasing to him.
> In the next place, [we learn] that righteousness and rectitude are a
> delight, but iniquity an abomination to him; and that, therefore,
> unless we will with impious ingratitude rebel against our Maker, we
> must necessarily spend our whole lives in the practice of righteous-
> ness. . . . Whatever he requires of us . . . we are under a *natural
> obligation* to obey.[1]

Calvin insists that *obligation* is rightly known only as to a Father
Lord, and that the master-servant model, a lower level of obligation, is inadequate. The genuine relation of man to his creator is
that of son to a father, not that of commanded to a sovereign. A
text from Malachi is a watchword for him here, and he seldom puts
this more richly than in a sermon on Genesis, chapter 22:

> The principal service that God demands is that we *love* him, for
> servile fear, when we tremble before his majesty and do unwillingly
> that which he commands, is nothing. God will reject all that. . . .
> He could have used the word *fear,* but this would not have been
> enough, because as I have already said we would serve God only
> halfway if we were motivated by the authority which he has over
> us. That would be only smoke. . . .
>
> He says by his prophet, "If I am your father, where is the love you
> should bear me? And if I am a master, where is my fear?" (Mal.
> 1:6). Especially does he attribute this term *love* to a *father.* Now
> he also puts in its turn the word master, but above all he names a
> father, and not without cause. For if we know God only as our
> superior it is certain that we will be motivated to serve him, but
> as I have already said, this will be only a servile fear.[2]

Note carefully, in anticipation of a contrary federal claim soon
to be made, that at no point in the divine economy are these "two
degrees of obligation"[3] separated. Calvin opens the *Institutes* (I,
ii) with the duty of man under "that first and simple knowledge,
to which the genuine order of nature would lead us, if Adam
had retained his innocence." He is speaking, he notes, not of the

knowledge of God as Redeemer, but of "the nature of pure and genuine religion" at the first and in general. Even here obligation for the natural man is unreservedly set beneath the fatherhood of God. "Persuaded of his goodness and mercy, he relies on him with unlimited confidence . . . Knowing him to be his *Lord* and *Father,* he concludes that he *ought* to mark his government in all things . . ." Such a man knows him as a "just Judge," but has no desire to evade his "justice," "because he loves and reveres God as his *Father,* honours and worships him as his *Lord,* and, even though there were no hell, would shudder at the thought of offending him."[4]

Calvin will often make this distinction: that God was known first as *Creator* and afterward and only by the elect as *Redeemer.* But he does not say, as we now see later theology so carefully say, that God was known first as *Creator Lord* and only afterward by the elect as *Father.* Some men, indeed, under law, fear God as lawgiver and judge and do not yet know him as father. But this is owing to the misconception of sin, for nowhere in the divine order does God reveal himself as Lord and lawgiver and not also as gracious father. Even in the self-manifestation of God in nature, so universally ignored, a divine father seeks his sons.

But the dialectic of covenants divorces these two degrees of obligation. The polar covenants obligate man differently because God is known differently in them. Turretin speaks for the later consensus as he notes the "characteristics in God as he contracts, who can be considered now as Creator and Lord, then as Redeemer and Father."[5] This "contracting" God binds differently. In the place of Calvin's one concept of obligation (save where it may inadequately be known), covenant theology has two, one for each covenant. So far as man is normally concerned, it is the law of the covenant of works, which "after his fall, continued to be a perfect rule of righteousness," that binds man to duty. The only use the Westminster Confession makes of the word "obligation" is in a paragraph which begins: "The moral law doth forever bind all . . . to the obedience thereof . . ."[6] The words "bind," "oblige," "duty," appear almost without exception in the context of the universal subjection of all to law.

The moral law is of use to all men, to inform them of the holy nature and will of God, and of their duty *binding* them to walk accordingly . . ."[7] [Larger Catechism]

A distinction between a *natural* and a *federal* obligation does nothing to alleviate this legalism. One simply reinforces the other.

Although man was already bound by a natural obligation as a rational creature, necessarily subject to the dominion of God and his law, yet he was more strongly bound by a *federal* obligation . . . by which each one is not only bound to obey the law but to fulfill it under the relation of a covenant to deserve eternal life.[8] [Turretin]

In both, man is a subject who serves "the Supreme Lawgiver, and the Chief Good"[9] (Witsius). Not until the arrival of the second, contrasting covenant is there any place established for obligation rising out of gratitude for paternal grace.

In the first covenant man was *bound* to do this in order that he might live, to deserve life, but in this [second covenant] he is *bound* to do the same, not that he may live but because he lives.[10]

Calvin had warned: "All the zeal that may be manifested by us in discharging our duty does not lay him under obligation to us by *any sort of merit;* for, as we are his property, so he on his part can owe us nothing."[11] But how hollow a Calvinist repetition of this becomes! The Calvinists cannot say it convincingly and effectively. If we ask them about man's natural obligation, we are levied with the discharge of a duty of works. If we ask Calvin, we get a contrary answer. Even if innocent we could not think of life as coming because man discharged his obligation. We discharge our duty precisely as we confess that we cannot discharge it. So Calvin argues in a sermon on Ephesians, chapter 5.

Inasmuch as we can bring God neither profit nor loss, he is content if we praise his name. For even if we should employ all our ability, what is in us with which God might be enriched or given some advantage? For he gives all things and needs nothing. It is an inestimable goodness to us that *he discharges us of all that we owe to him in return for our affirming that we are bound and obligated to him and that we cannot discharge ourselves of it. Then if we come in all humility to him to confess the obligation that we have to God, this and nothing more is the payment that he requires of us.*[12]

Life, notes Calvin finely and perhaps surprisingly, is a continual Sabbath.

2. Man's Accountability

Man's generic accountability is devastatingly clear in the Westminster Confession. The race of men are at the start established in "a covenant of works, wherein life was promised to Adam, and in him to his posterity, upon condition of perfect and personal obedience," and at the end, with this covenant universally (though not exclusively) valid still, are called "to give an account of their thoughts, words, and deeds . . . to receive according to what they have done in the body . . ."[13] Herman Bavinck describes this "share" in the getting of life which belonged to man originally and which yet has a certain perpetual validity:

> Then the rule held: Do this and thou shalt live. By way of perfect obedience to God's command he was to set about inheriting eternal life. In itself that was a good way . . . And God has not, on His part, broken that rule. He still holds to it. If there were a man who could perfectly keep God's law, he would still receive eternal life as his reward.[14]

For Ames this "required perfect obedience of works, which was to be performed by man with his own strength."[15] For Turretin, in it life "rests upon the work of man."[16]

But had these two paragraphs from Calvin's Sermons on Ephesians and Sermons on Job, preached at Geneva, been heard and heeded at Westminster, there never would have been a covenant of works, with its novel notion of man's accountability, and the course of Reformed theology would have been far more faithful to the mind of Calvin. These alone suffice to establish the argument we have been developing throughout this book, and to show amply how far the Westminster Confession went astray from the Reformed faith Calvin had committed to his church:

> Let us put the case that we were in the integrity in which our father Adam was at the first. Should we then presume it was of ourselves under the illusion that God had ennobled us in this way? Now we hold everything from him. . . . Would we have it through our own dexterity? Would we have got it by our own strength? [vertu, power] No! But we would have it because God had given it to us through his own free goodness.[17]

> Let us recognize then that the praise is due to him that we may not defraud him of that which belongs to him. *For if we should live as perfectly as angels and yet have the foolish idea that this came from our own free will and of our own movement, then we would miss the principal thing.* To what end serve all our good works lest it be that God in them is glorified. *But if we think ourselves the author of them, we see that they are corrupted in so doing, and are converted into vices,* so that they are nothing more than ambition.[18]

Indeed! Had Calvin been a member of the Westminster Assembly, he would have been first to cast his vote against the Confession, and to register protest that its doctrine of man was scandalous. Far from being God's original plan for man, this notion of a man able to render account for himself is that which natural man assumes in sin. The folly of man is ever his thinking himself able to do this and that with his own wisdom, free will, and virtue. Westminster's portrait of man, normative though it is and despoiled in the fall, is that portrait of man which Calvin incessantly denounces as pagan and diabolical, whether claimed for him ideally or actually.

> The Holy Spirit here wishes to thunder out against this opinion with which the world has always been drunk, that is, of free will. For the pagans knew enough to say that God had indeed created them in the world, and that he was able to give them good fortune, as they termed it. But they held that each had it in his hand and in his own choosing to follow virtue, and walk so that no fault might be found in him.
>
> See then how the pagans divided things between God and themselves: the latter matter, that is, putting us here below to crawl about like frogs, they gave to God, but they said that attaining to heaven was the ability [*faculté*] of man. . . . We can cooperate, so they say, so that when it comes to the reckoning [*conte, compte*], the principal part will be found in us.[19]

> Such is the wicked ambition which belongs to our nature, that when the question relates to the origin of our salvation, we quickly form diabolical imaginations about our own merits.[20]

Calvin excludes every suggestion of a meritorious and grateful acknowledgement which renders efficacious the grace of God.[21]

Think of man as accountable, pleads Calvin, only under the governing principle of God's grace. Man does not present an account of his accomplishments and look for felicity on grounds of the profit, fruition, or increase of his talents. He does not achieve but rather receives felicity. The part that is given to man is a dependent, subordinate accountability. Man is called to account for his acknowledging or not acknowledging the blessing of God. On this basis he forfeits or retains life. From literally hundreds of passages that well illustrate Calvin's thought here, the following must suffice as typical:

> Our Lord calls us gently to him, he wishes to win us by such kindness, and therefore if we do not deign to come to him that which we receive at his hand will cost us right dearly. *It is true that God asks no payment from us, for we can bring him nothing. But yet as our duty he would have us render an expression of thanksgiving to him. If we do not do this, the sacrilege must be laid to our charge that we have ravaged the blessings of God, for being in no way his children.* For what right do we have to enjoy them unless it is that he is our father? . . . What remains but that our Lord enter into account [*entrer en conte*] with us, if we on our part do not desire to serve him, and if the ease and rest which he has given us is not applied to the end that we truly show that we hold him for our father, inasmuch as he treats us as his children. If, I say, we do not acknowledge this, then our ingratitude will not go unpunished.[22]

Under God, life is not of works; life is of grateful leisure, ease, and rest. Sin dis-eases and puts us to work.

3. Man's Ability

That man is accountable involves not only a notion of an account he is to render, but also of an ability to do so. Calvin considers, often at length, the question of human ability. His vocabulary is that of *ability* or *faculty* (*facultas, faculté*) and of *virtue* or *strength* (*virtus, vertu*), and closely related is the extended debate about the will of man. But because he sees all ability as a gracious gift from God, he is inclined, especially when not drawn into controversy, to speak more of man's gifts or talents than of his abilities.

The question of man's ability is reducible in Calvin to that of man's will. Here Calvin's vocabulary is that of *will* (*voluntas*), and the somewhat different *arbitrium* (choice, or will), with related words such as *electio* (choice). In modern analysis of responsibility, questions of will and of ability may be kept distinct; man may be willing but unable to do something, or he may be able and unwilling. But such is the subordination in Calvin of both will and ability to God's grace and power that the two questions dissolve into one. When sifted out of his debate, Calvin's whole orientation here shows how closely he desires to tie the human will to divine grace, and it is especially fruitful to follow the case of integral man.

When pressed by critics in argument, Calvin twists and turns but is willing to grant that man in integrity had a "faculty of choosing" or "the power of his own determination," an ability which he does not now have. If Calvin were to say no more, his concessions could form a point of departure for unfolding a concept of ability such as that the Westminster divines were to develop. Faced by opponents with a passage from Ecclesiasticus, he concedes the point that in the Genesis portrait man had some choice, but maintains that he lost it.

> The writer [of Ecclesiasticus] says, that man, as soon as he was created, was left in the power of his own determination [*in manu consilii sui*]; that precepts were given to him, which if he kept, he should also be kept by them; that he had life and death, good and evil, set before him; and that whatever he desired, would be given him. Let it be granted, that man at his creation was endowed with the faculty of choosing [*facultas adipiscendae*] life or death. What if we reply, that he has lost it?[23]

Calvin may term this *free will* more to please his critics than to suit his own systemic needs. It was open to man then whether he should live or die. It was up to him. He did then choose, and he could have done otherwise than he did do. Such passages in Calvin, especially when addressed to a philosophical audience, allow the reading in of a concept of man endowed with a deposit of powers and subsequently left to obtain eternal life by their right use.

> The primitive condition of man was ennobled with these eminent faculties; he possessed reason, understanding, prudence, and judgment, not only for the government of his life on earth, but to enable him to ascend even to God and eternal felicity. To these was added choice [*electio*], to direct the appetites, and regulate all the organic motions; so that the will [*voluntas*] should be entirely conformed to the government of reason. In this integrity man was

endued with free will [*liberum arbitrium*], by which, if he had wished, he might have chosen eternal life.[24]

But what Calvin momentarily seems to grant, he can swiftly retract. Or, more accurately, he grants to primal man a power of choosing life only in oscillation with the assertion that in such choice he would have been empowered by God. "He had received the power, indeed, if he chose to exert it . . ."[25] Calvin is always uncomfortable with admissions such as those just cited, lest the conclusion follow that this primitive endowment was such that should man have chosen the good he would have cause for self-congratulation. This power of choosing is but the power to answer the call of grace. Seldom is Calvin content to terminate such an exchange without a warning to his critics lest they use his concessions to drive a wedge between human action and divine grace. Uneasy about what is taught in the Ecclesiasticus passage, for instance, Calvin will not leave it without making it clear that he does not license for man in integrity or for man now such a free will as to have any ability for self-salvation. He replies

> . . . to Ecclesiasticus himself, whoever he be: If you design to teach man to seek within himself a power [*facultas*] to attain salvation, your authority is not so great in our estimation as to obtain even the smallest degree of credit, in opposition to the undoubted word of God.[26]

One has ever to recall the radical cautions of the Commentary on Genesis, where even in integrity man seeks all life in "divine grace," and "lives not by his own power [*virtus*], but by the kindness of God alone," claiming "nothing for himself as if it were his own." Any seeming exaltation of man has to be tempered with the humility of the Sermons on Ephesians, recently cited. Else all is lost. "If we should live as perfectly as angels and yet have the foolish idea that this came from our own free will and of our own movement, then we would miss the principal thing. . . . If we think ourselves the author of [our works], . . . they are corrupted in so doing, and are converted into vices." Any "faculty of choosing" with which man is endowed is not a *power in himself*, but a *power in God*. Man in integrity was given to will, but not autonomously so; he was given rightly to will theonomously in address by divine grace, a *power in grace* which acts as it rests on the objective necessity of God's indwelling presence. The human will is always to be circumscribed and funded by divine power.

Calvin uses here (and to some extent modifies) the Augustinian distinction between *arbitrium* (will, choice) and *voluntas* (will). Man has a faculty of willing (*voluntas*), but it is only when this will is enclosed by grace that man makes a choice (*arbitrium*) of the good. Positively, Calvin is simply not an indeterminist or libertarian in his concept of man, even in integrity. The desire for a free will (*liberum arbitrium*) is the root sin, which "cast down the human race" and forever enslaves it, and Calvin is regularly vituperative toward it.[27] His freedom for integral man is nearer that of a theological soft determinism, where man is both free and yet determined by divine grace, without incompatibility. Yet, negatively, there is asymmetry. We may forsake the grace of God in favor of free will. If so, the choice (*arbitrium*) of the will (*voluntas*) brings not freedom but rather death. The will turns on itself and becomes concupiscent, or self-willed. "We must take care that the grace of God is not darkened as we think ourselves to have done this or that. It is necessary then that men attribute nothing at all to themselves."[28] The denial of free will—let this register fully—is a consequence not so much of the power of God as of his grace.

But what is understood when the Westminster Confession, Chapter XI, "Of Free Will," teaches for Calvinism a century later that "Man, in his state of innocency, had *freedom* and *power* to *will* and to *do* that which is good and well-pleasing to God"? What must be concluded about the kind of ability Adam, the type of our genus, once had when the Confession proceeds to the statement that man has "lost all ability of will to any spiritual good accompanying salvation," and "is not able, by his own strength, to convert himself, or to prepare himself thereunto"? Is it not that man is no longer able to do this "by his own strength," but that once, by the norm of his destiny in creation, he was so able? Such endowment must accompany the first covenant, and the Confession posits for this normative man "power and ability to keep it."[29] Since this general covenant is carefully defined as being not of grace but of works, can we escape the conclusion that man was first to do (and normally yet held responsible for not doing) "by his own strength" what later God covenants in grace to do for his elect? Where Calvin envelopes all human ability in grace, covenant theology now divorces man's ability and God's grace.

This is not offset by the attempts of covenant theology to wrestle with the problem. The federal divines never quite forgot that this primitive ability of man was an endowment from God, and they knew that God needs to preserve and sustain these gifts. Witsius speaks with representative caution of any intrinsic independence:

> God gave to man the charge of this his image, as the most excellent deposit of heaven, and, if kept pure and inviolate, the earnest of a greater good; for that end he endowed him with sufficient powers from his very formation, so as to stand in need of no other habitual grace. It was only requisite that God, by the continual influx of his providence, should preserve those powers, and excite them to all and each of their acts. For, there can be no state conceived in which the creature can act independently of the Creator; not excepting the angels themselves, though now confirmed in holiness and happiness.[30]

Turretin too reserves place for "the help of God, both to actuate these faculties and powers and to preserve them from change."[31]

But with due allowance for the reservation that man is not altogether independent, the federalists know a point where man, at least in the noble representative of his kind, needs no further grace beyond this habitual or minimum endowment, but is to proceed alone on his own strength of will to a higher good. In the words of the Westminster Confession, man and woman are "left to the liberty of their own will."[32] This must be so, because in some sense man and not God must be the responsible author of good works, if man is to attain salvation by creditable performance. Even if it is God-given ability, it is man's right use of this ability. Even if it is God-instituted freedom, it is man's righteous use of this freedom. We cannot avoid the implication that should this man whom God has "left" to the liberty of his own will succeed with these powers on deposit, he primarily, and not the God who left him so, is the responsible one. If the God who once left him to the exercise of his own abilities returns at length to establish a covenant of grace additionally to the covenant of works, this does not alter the normative conception of what it means to be a responsible man.

Admittedly, Calvin may vacillate: here man has a primitive faculty of willing with which to ascend to God; there this willing and ascending is enveloped by grace. But there is no violence or inconsistency in this vacillation; it is readily soluble: all ability is response-ability to grace. Not even in Calvin, we should concede, is it soluble without residue, for questions of responsibility have a remarkable resistance to dissolution. But orthodoxy cannot solve, but can only compound and deepen, the problem with its self-reliant responsible man.

4. Man's Responsibility

In the Reformation heritage, God has taken upon himself unendingly a certain responsibility for man. This means immediately that man is not independently responsible but is allocated responsibility only within creaturehood and sonship. In his own gracious freedom, God chose to create man, to place him in an earthly paradise (real for the Reformers, however problematic in the twentieth century), to give him the hope and inheritance of eternal life, and to promise ever to care for man. Even after man in irresponsibility forfeited and corrupted these riches, God did not forsake his responsibility toward man. He rather chose to deepen his obligation; his grace has superabounded and assumed the new obligation of providing for man's redemption and restoration. In creation and again, more richly, in redemption, man is to find life as he receives it from the hand of another, a free gift from one who is his Lord, his master, and above all his father. God has for man an unqualified good will, boundless and unlimited, an *agape* which is oblivious to merit and desert. Man has a responsible God.

That man is a son of God implies the essential relationship of dependence written into his order of existence. It defines him as one who does not stand alone, neither entirely nor in some part, but as one who abides in and draws strength and security from another. This means that man is given a reciprocal responsibility circumscribed by a larger relationship of another's being responsible for him. He is not, was not, and is not destined to be an autonomous agent selecting what is good for himself, depending on his own willpower to bring him the good life, living by his works, making himself pleasing to God. However exciting and mature this may seem, it is for Calvin a certain route into slavery. The man who thinks to determine his works finds that his works determine him. This is what man tried to accomplish in sin, to assume primary responsibility for himself. He "strove to raise himself up apart from the Lord." But the Christian faith explodes all this. Man is not made for responsible independence. He is made for responsible co-respondence. Responsibility is not "in" him but "in" this dialogue. He is not made for individualism, but rather for unbroken union and communion with God.

But sons do have a responsibility. There is nothing we can or need do for ourselves that we may earn our father's good pleasure. That we already have. But his very love and care for us gives us something that we must do. We are to express our gratitude. We are given to "retain" the life with which we are gifted by "acknowledging that it is received from God." In Adam, and again in Christ, men are given a subordinate and derived responsibility. Man may accept, or reject, his father's love. This is not a small, or an unreal, or an immature responsibility restricted by an overprotective father. That man needs God and lives not independently but abiding in him is ennobling, not demeaning, as is also, for instance, his need for friendship and family on the human plane. This frees him to love with a joyous heart, to be at leisure from works in a continual Sabbath, certain of his status, that he may become what he is. So responsibility is transvalued. Responsible autonomy, the fugitive dream of sin, is an irresponsible slavery. Responsible correspondence in God is perfect freedom. It frees for what is the chief end of man: to glorify God and enjoy him forever.

CHAPTER 7

Irresponsible Man:
His Culpability

This responsible man may also be irresponsible. It is next our concern that he has been and is so. He will not allow another to be responsible for him; unfaithful, disobedient, unbelieving, concupiscent, and ungrateful, he insists on assuming immediate responsibility for himself. We have now to explore this. Calvin maintains that God has been and is responsible in proffering man his care at every point. But man culpably ignores him, blinded by his delusions of autonomous responsibility. This question is especially acute at the point of the natural man in his sin, and an analysis of Calvin's position here is correspondingly clarifying and rewarding. His account, we shall find, was predictably garbled by the Westminster divines.

1. Culpable Ignorance

We should perhaps first acknowledge that Calvin concedes that the natural man is not charged unreservedly with full responsibility for his ignorance. "The heathen will have some excuse in part, though not in whole, for still their sin is not so grievous or so horrible before God, because they have had no doctrine."[1] They will be judged in the context of the light available to them by the God we know in Christ. We could develop this further, but what interests us now is the extent of their culpability. And Calvin holds that this excuse is never total; there is always blame. That they had no doctrine is more their fault than God's; theirs is a sin of neglect.

> The pretext of ignorance made by unbelievers is wholly vain. There are those who on the first view seem to be excusable for

their error, as they have not been taught, and never understood who the true God is; but yet there is in them the blame of neglect as well as of wickedness, for they wilfully neglect and despise the only true God.[2]

Calvin holds that man may reasonably be held responsible for his ignorance. Man has ignored God's invitation in nature. We have already seen in chapter 2 how Calvin's writings abound with the teaching that an essentially complete knowledge of God is immediately available to all. He cannot overstate the objective clarity of this self-declaration. But this adequate knowledge does not reach subjectivity in man. Man resists, ignores it. This is responsible ignorance, which Calvin, following Paul in Romans 1—2 and in Acts, connects inseparably with ingratitude. Ingratitude blinds man, he is ignorant of God, but "ignorance proceeds from a sinful disposition of the mind."

> To enjoy everything in nature without acknowledging the Author of the benefit, is the basest ingratitude. . . . they . . . will one day feel the force of the expression of Paul, related by Luke, that God has not left himself ἀμάρτυρον, without witness. For they shall not be permitted to escape with impunity because they have been deaf and insensible to testimonies so illustrious. And, in truth, it is the part of *culpable ignorance* [*maligna ignorantia*], never to see God, who everywhere gives signs of his presence. . . . They were culpably ignorant of God, only because they were voluntarily and culpably blinded.[3]

There are four points of emphasis here. (1) God is both graciously and adequately knowable. God is defined in his creatures no differently from the definition of Exodus 34: "The Lord, the Lord God, merciful and gracious, long suffering, and abundant in goodness and truth, keeping mercy for thousands, forgiving iniquity, and transgression, and sin . . ." None of his perfections is omitted. So runs the argument of the *Institutes,* I, x. (2) What man is invited and required to do is not essentially different from man's original duty or, *mutatis mutandis,* what is asked of him when the gospel comes. Again, the *Institutes,* I, x, is quite explicit:

> The knowledge of God, which is afforded us in the Scriptures, is designed for the same end as that which we derive from the creatures: it invites us first to the fear of God, and then to con-

fidence in him; that we may learn to honour him with perfect
innocence of life, and sincere obedience to his will, and to place all
our dependence on his goodness.[4]

We insist on these claims in Calvin, in anticipation of the fact that
a century later the Westminster Confession cannot make them,
but invites the natural man to his God differently than is done
in the biblical invitation.

(3) Man's guilt is epitomized in his doing precisely the opposite of what he is asked, and so he repeats the primal ingratitude.
It is a sin of omission, but one which is fired by his independence.
(4) Yet in the process there is a fundamental heedlessness. Men
do what they do blindly, oblivious of God's grace, like arrogant
and spoiled children. Like the unrighteous in Jesus' parable of the
sheep and the goats, they sin ignorantly, but ignorance is evidence
of their self-centeredness. The problem is complicated by the fact
that men do come to a false knowledge of God, which supposes
him to be served to their credit in legal obedience. On this Calvin
also bases an auxiliary responsibility, which we presently examine.
But of the true and gracious God, they remain responsibly ignorant.

Calvin's chief obstacle to plausibility is of course the disarray
of the natural world, problematic enough in the sixteenth century,
to say nothing of the twentieth. Is it a sober reading of the natural
order to argue that God speaks so graciously and plainly there?
Calvin is sensitive to this point, and that he concedes some partial
excuse to the natural man shows his realism. But he insists on a
kind of natural idealism. That we see so little proves no inadequacy in God's self-revelation, but rather how sin clouds the mind.
An exemplary religious viewing of nature is not found in the
alienated natural man, but in Jesus, who, with eyes undimmed
by sin, found omnipresent evidences of a father's solicitude in
earth, sky, field, and flower. It is by considering the lilies that we
ought to be led to faith. This is not a naïveté unmindful of the
elements of evil and tragedy now commingled in the natural order,
but one which can penetrate through them to a father's heart, to
the ideal order of nature distinct from yet hidden in the present
course of nature. Calvin develops this in the various passages in

Psalms, Acts, Romans, Corinthians, etc., which give him opportunity. The Commentary on Acts is representative:

> They fly to this fortress: that they ought to bear no blame, but rather God was without feeling who did not even condescend to give so much as a hoot to call back those that he saw were perishing. . . . [But] God was hidden in such a way that all the while he bore witness to himself. . . . He did not permit, so far as he could, the world to err. . . . In the order of nature there is a certain and evident manifestation of God . . . but they went about by culpable and barbarous ingratitude to erase the glory of God, in which they betrayed their impudence.[5]

> Surely there is nothing more absurd than that men should ignore their author, who are endowed with understanding principally for this use. We must especially note the goodness of God as he so familiarly thrusts himself upon us that even the blind may grope after him. For this reason the blindness of man is more shameful and less tolerable, who in so clear and evident a manifestation are touched with no feeling of God's presence. Wherever they cast their eyes they must necessarily see lively and also innumerable images of divine power, wisdom, and goodness. For God has not darkly shadowed his glory in the creation of the world, but he has everywhere engraved such clear marks that even blind men may know them by groping. From this we conclude that men are not only blind but stupid as well, when being helped by such excellent testimonies, they make no progress . . .
> Being void of right judgment, they pass over without understanding all such signs of God's glory as appear clearly both in heaven and on earth. . . . They are inexcusable when they are blind in such clear light. . . . Therefore, though men's senses fail them in seeking out God, yet they have no pretext to cover their guilt, because though he offers himself to be handled and groped, they continue all the same in bewilderment.[6]

The objection will persist that man did not really have the ability to perceive this God who "familiarly thrusts himself upon us" and "offers himself to be handled and groped." Here Calvin's most consistent answer is that in quite an important sense no "ability" is required. But to that we return, for first we must recognize that Calvin can also answer that ability is needed and that it has been lost. When he so argues, he would make it perfectly clear that man cannot make his way to God.

St. Paul says that the natural man is not able to understand the things of the Spirit. He does not say that men are so froward that they *will* not understand; but he says that they cannot understand at all; the *faculty* [*faculté*] and the *power* [*vertu*] is not in us. Why? Because of the corruption which has come upon us through the sin of Adam.[7]

For this matter we lack not merely inclination [*voluntas,* will] but ability [*facultas*].[8]

Yet also to a certain extent he argues the point *ad hominem,* in terms of his opponents' philosophical analysis of man. To the contention that men have some ability to discover God, Calvin replies that they do not. They did have, but lost it.

We cannot forget here, though, that we have already inquired what ability Calvin allows to man in integrity and found that such ability is enveloped in grace. It misleads us and amplifies the problem to say that this lost ability was independent of alliance with divine grace. Ability and will are interconnected, and if Calvin can sometimes disconnect them, he can also unambiguously reconnect them. What is needed by the natural man, reminiscent of integral man, is as much a faculty of will as a faculty distinguishable from will. As man will not, he disables himself. No independent ability is requisite. All the ability man needs is an inclination to receive; any inclination is immediately sufficient ability, for were man but receptive, God would fulfill the requirements of communication. It is certainly not Calvin's intent to suggest that man needs a faculty to be so employed that an able man and not an enabling God is responsible or even partially responsible for his successful knowing and living. Once man has assumed any ability apart from grace, we recall, he has fallen into sin.

The following rather remarkable passage from the Sermons on Ephesians reflects the spirit of Calvin here. God offers himself to us in his works. But we are dazzled and fall into an abyss, wholly unable to understand. Why? The trouble is that when *we think ourselves able* to actively search out God, we are wholly unable. But if we would let *him teach us,* passively receiving what he wishes to reveal, we should have understanding enough, we should be able.

Someone will here ask, however, How then can we confess God to be righteous, wise, and almighty, if we are so dazzled by his works? For you say that it is the wisdom of men to inquire after the works of God and to apply all their diligence to them, and that this is also why he has ordered the world to be as a theatre in which we ought to contemplate his goodness, righteousness, power, and wisdom. Therefore, there seems to be some contrariety here: that we are to be diligent and attentive in considering the works of God, and yet at the same time that our understanding vanishes away when we think upon them.

But the solution to this is easy: If we should desire with sobriety to know these things which God wishes to reveal to us, and which are useful to us, *we should have understanding enough;* and we should indeed learn that he has no desire at all that we should not be taught by his works to come to him and put our trust in knowing how to invoke him, to discern between good and evil, to walk according to his will. We should then in all the works of God understand all the things that are useful for our salvation, if we did not give rein to our foolish and disordered lusts, but behaved as pupils who waited for that which it pleased their master to show them. This is why it is said in the book of Job (chapter 26) that we would do well if we should see the fringes of the works of God. *We would be able then* to taste the wisdom and righteousness, power and goodness of God, as we considered only the fringes of his works. But if we wish profoundly to sound them out, we will find this abyss mentioned before, which is able to swallow up all our understanding.[9]

The problem is man's attitude, not his aptitude. Had the former been right, the latter would have sufficed. The wrongness of this disabling attitude consists in man's presuming for himself an aptitude which was never his. If there is a certain lost ability in Calvin, which renders man unable to appreciate God in his works, it is equally true that it is man's willful claiming of an unwarranted ability that thwarts his hearing God in nature. If there is an ability required, there is also a kind and an interpretation of ability neither required nor allowed.

God's word in nature is as his word in gospel. Put the case that man did respond to the natural invitation. It would not be in his own strength, any more than it is so when man answers the gospel calling. It is the elusive thing that though Calvin seems to leave place for something man is to supply, the righteous man always knows that God supplies all ability, he enables and man claims nothing. Yet there is asymmetry. When man ignores God's natural invitation, his guilt is of the same order, though not of the same degree, as the man who is heedless of the gospel. God has not failed him, but he resists the Spirit. If we have followed Calvin faithfully, the problem of responsibility is one under nature or gospel. The natural man's culpability is not so much his wanting in able works (as the Westminster Confession must say), as it is his thwarting of divine grace.

This account of responsibility is far from being problem free. It has at its center an asymmetry which for Calvin is ineradicable. Responsible man is so in correspondence with divine grace; in his responsibility he can claim nothing for himself, but must rest in his union with God. Irresponsible man is so in culpable ignorance of divine grace; his responsibility is his own—he has severed himself from God. But this asymmetry is perennial in religious thought so far as the concept of grace is seriously entertained, and is by no means peculiar to Calvin.

2. Conscience and the Law of Nature

While man knows neither his primary responsibility nor his sin, he does come to a secondary type of conviction of wrongdoing, which Calvin considers sufficient to render him inexcusable. We here examine responsibility not so much as it actually and ultimately is, but as it may be argued from the side of man, in the light which breaks through to him. We have already sketched in Calvin a "naturally engraven righteousness of the law." This passage is representative of Calvin's use of that law to hold man responsible.

> Because it might appear absurd that the Gentiles should perish without any previous knowledge, he [Paul] immediately subjoins that their conscience supplies in the place of a law to them, and it is therefore sufficient for their just condemnation. The end of the law of nature, therefore, is, that man may be rendered inexcusable. Nor will it be improperly defined in this manner—That it is a sentiment of the conscience sufficiently discerning between good and evil, to deprive men of the pretext of ignorance, while they are convicted even by their own testimony.[10]

This must be related to man's primary responsibility with care, especially in the light of the confusion introduced by later development in Reformed thought.

Students of Calvin have noticed, often critically, how he can say in the same breath that this is and is not a knowledge of God. Virtually every statement that men have knowledge sufficient to be without excuse concludes with the somewhat contradictory reservation that this is in fact no real knowledge at all.

> We receive a slight perception of his divinity, sufficient to render us inexcusable. Accordingly, when Paul here declares [in 1 Corinthians] that God is not known through means of his creatures, you must understand him to mean that a pure knowledge of him is not attained. For that none may have any pretext for ignorance, mankind make proficiency in the universal school of nature so far as to be affected with some perception of deity, but what God is, they know not, nay more, they straightway become vain in their imaginations.[11]

But there is a fairly clear rationale behind this prima facie inconsistency. Though men know God exists and asks to be served, in sinful self-will and presumption they mistake his character. Deceived with false ideas of righteousness, man believes that heaven or hell depends on whether he has demonstrated himself worthy or unworthy, good or bad. What has a certain similitude of righteousness is but the shell of virtue, because it is done self-confidently, while true virtue springs from grateful acknowledgment of grace by the man whose confidence is not in self but in God.

When sin enters, it transforms responsibility. Instead of man's resting in his responsible God, now in his independence man assumes responsibility for himself. He arrogates to himself and invents his own responsibility. Seeking to guarantee his well-being through virtue, man traces the law on his heart back to its divine origin and becomes deluded, his chief delusion being that his religion makes place more for glorifying man than for praising God. Even in obeying law, man is not celebrating the goodness of God, but demonstrating his own goodness.

> Pagans have always wished to be acceptable to God by their own virtues. . . . The heathens fully believed that they would be rewarded by God if they lived in honest and unblamable fashion among men.[12]
>
> God does not wish to entertain men with some confidence or trust in their merits, for we are too much given to this by nature.

We have seen it is an error which has been common in all the world and throughout all time. It is not necessary that we go to school to persuade ourselves that we are a capable race and that by our virtue we can obligate God to us.[13]

It is this delusion, radically wrong as it is, that God uses to hold man responsible. This false idea of righteousness arises in sin, yet notwithstanding God gives it a certain sanction. He lets it be a naturally engraven righteousness of the law. This is not what God wants for man, nor is it all he offers, for we do not forget how also and primarily God speaks graciously to man in nature. But the man whom he cannot reach with his gracious word he does reach with this accommodation of law to the sinful notion of man. The man who is already but ignorantly inexcusable for resisting God's gracious invitation in nature, now in this further way is made consciously inexcusable. God lets him be responsible as he is wont to be, to show him irresponsible in this way too. Just as Israel, though it had God's evangelical promise to Abraham, persisted in stubborn ignorance of both its duty and its sin until God added the legal Mosaic promise, so too the natural world has a twofold level of responsibility. To God's natural fatherly invitation, which holds man responsible yet fails to produce conscious conviction of sin, is added a natural law which can successfully so convict.

It is a vain excuse if someone allege: "Ho, now, I am not a scholar." For there are things that our Lord has engraven in men so that they have been taught as it were from their mother's womb. . . . We need no word of God to condemn them, they can allege no ignorance of religion, for nature should lead them to it. . . . "Ho, well, I was never instructed in the gospel." And were you never taught a sufficient doctrine by nature? Did you not know how to discern between good and bad, as Paul puts it? Have we not a sufficient knowledge to convict us in the last day and prove that we merit condemnation?[14]

When men sin against this law, in self-deception they become "doubly blind," sharing in the first instance that ignoring of God's paternal call which is congenital to all men, and entering as well into a further blindness where even the commonly perceived moral order is suppressed.

In the legal, Mosaic promise, God teaches what he requires, diffracted through the sinful disposition of man. In one sense he does, and in another he does not, teach man what his responsibility actually is. So with God's law on the heart. This legal, natural responsibility is and yet is not what God asks. There is a coloring of God's requirements with man's vanity. It is what is left of God's requirements when sin shuts out the proffered grace of God and lets through only law, a darkened, legalized responsibility. Though man has no inkling of a beneficent God whom he has but to acknowledge, depend on, and gratefully receive (invited to this, he ignores it), yet God accepts, even sanctions his mistaken sense of responsibility, and uses his notion of virtuous self-salvation to hold him culpable. Guilt here is an ethical guilt where the natural man is unaware of his primal concupiscence and yet recognizes that he has not kept the moral law. In this double responsibility the latter may be more practical and plausible, but the former is basic. There may be a law within man. But primarily there is grace without him, surrounding and confronting him. There are things about his ultimate responsibility of which the irresponsible moral man never dreams.

Received Reformed apologetics customarily omits what is for Calvin the basic half of this argument, then garbles the remainder. Under the double covenant pattern, for man to be without excuse, it is necessary only that the details of the first covenant be given in nature. There is neither place nor need for a God who in nature graciously offers himself to man and invites all to that order of responsibility which is set out later under the gospel covenant. The reason grace is not known in nature is not, as with Calvin, that it is ignored, but because it is not proclaimed to man there.

Turretin debates this at length and concludes that natural culpability can only be legal.

> The question is . . . whether there is a real call through the works of nature by which all are summoned to the covenant of grace. This we deny. . . . Whatever the revelation of nature may be, it differs not only in degree but in species from the revelation of the word.

It is pointed out to Turretin that in indictment of the Gentile world, "Paul . . . regards them not as . . . guilty of having violated the first covenant alone," but makes them "guilty of having despised and most contemptuously rejected kindness." Turretin confidently answers, *Not so,* for if this is true, "we must ascribe to the voice of nature and of the creatures the preaching of the divine mercy manifested in Christ alone by the Scriptures." This cannot be the case, else the whole federal system would topple. The natural man had no revelation of the divine mercy; God's goodness was only somewhat known, after the manner of a covenant of works. The normal man has no other covenant to violate.

> There is no mortal who is not by nature under the covenant of works, as each individual bears the work of the law, which is the contract of that covenant, written on his conscience. . . . As the former was made in the state of nature, so it was known by nature, and impressed upon the consciences of men, in which the work of the law was written (Rom. 2:14-15). But the second is a mystery entirely hidden, unless it is made known to us by a supernatural revelation.[15]

In this light we must understand the Westminster Confession's opening claim that the light of nature teaches enough of God to leave man without excuse, but on the other hand does not teach saving knowledge of God.

> Although the light of nature, and the works of creation and providence, do so far manifest the goodness, wisdom, and power of God, as to leave men inexcusable; yet they are not sufficient to give that knowledge of God, and of his will, which is necessary unto salvation . . .[16]

Students of the Confession have frequently complained that there is an asymmetry here; knowledge of God sufficient to judge would seem to the uninitiated to be knowledge of God sufficient to save. But this is not so at all of the Confession's presuppositions, and the Confession, however it may have misunderstood Calvin, is internally consistent. The light of nature teaches law and natural covenant which for fallen man can only judge, but grace is unknown except to believers. This may be seen clearly when the opening claim is put with chapters VII and XXI (or XIX) on the covenants and on divine law. The light of nature which the Westminster standards frequently invoke is that of the first covenant under which all men are born and live and by which all except the elect will be judged. Culpability may and ought to be based on this covenant alone, for man's responsibility is naturally knowable and more or less naturally known. In man's present fallen state, this cannot save, but that is of no consequence for its power to condemn. So Reformed apologetics pursued man's natural culpability with considerable rationalistic zeal. On this point the gospel gave it nothing further to say.

Once again, as repeatedly in our study, beneath similarities between Calvin and the Calvinists lie very basic differences. They concur that man's conscience and moral sense serves as a naturally engraven righteousness of the law. But what for Calvin involves a distorted mixing of truth and error, God's will and man's sinful fancy, has now been put in a different status. This righteousness of the law is man's correct sensing of the standard of responsibility for which he was made. It is as true for Calvin as for the Confession that man ought to obey the law of nature, and as true for each that obedience is impossible. But despite this parallelism, what is for Calvin really man's notion of how he ought to be responsible, and God's responsibility for him only as God reaches through sin to hold man responsible on his own terms, has in the Confession become precisely and fully what man ought to do. Calvin's diabolical idea of a God who invites men to self-salvation has reached confessional status as the normal, natural, and correct relation between man and his God.

The problem of ability now becomes acute. This problem is not absent from Calvin, but is soluble in the enabling grace of God. Or at least the problem of ability is reducible to the question of will: God will graciously enable, if man but will allow him. Then there is residual paradox. Under the federal natural order there is no such resolution. Additionally to the problem of what man will do, there is that of what he can do. Man is in need of some aptitude to search out God in his law and some capacity to obey it. Since this ability of the first covenant is lost, is it just for God to hold man culpable accordingly? Reformed thought has insisted, lost ability notwithstanding, that all men are culpable for default of the general covenant. But it has done so without much creditability.

The Confession condemns us because we have brought nothing right to God; Calvin reprimands because we have taken nothing rightly from God. The Confession makes man an unprofitable servant. Calvin finds him a poor steward, or even more, an ungrateful son, who, when he tries to be a profitable servant, fails in that as well.

CHAPTER 8
Reformed Responsible Man

The reader has doubtless reacted to our argument by wondering if, for all its interest as historical theology, the issue is not largely archaic, since the myth of the primitive covenants with Adam has long since collapsed and become incredible. The Westminster standards, where they yet remain as official documents, are admittedly dated, but that renders them on these matters innocuous. To react so is perhaps understandable, especially since we have chosen to argue largely in terms that Calvin and the Calvinists took literally but that we must now consider mythological.

But no claim of orthodoxy demythologized as readily as the doctrine of the covenants, and hence none was revalidated as successfully when Reformed theology moved into the modern era. When the literalism of the first covenant was refined away, under the pressure of criticism in the nineteenth and twentieth centuries, this concept of a responsible man tended nonetheless to remain. Man finds himself, whatever the means of his arrival here, with a deposit of abilities and under divine law; these determine his self-understanding and his responsibilities. The historical covenant is replaced with timeless divine-natural truths. The man who is now infected with sin cannot save himself; on this there was an insistent consensus. But this in no way affects the normative (if no longer primal or original) concept of responsibility. The view of man in relation to God that the Westminster Confession entertains, save for its modification for believers, is essentially rationalist or philosophical or "natural," as Calvin knew so well, and it was readily accommodated to an increasingly rationalistic age.

Representative quasi-official statements from recent Reformed theology should leave no doubt of the continuing federal presence. Consider, for instance, though the twin covenants are gone, how subtly the long shadow of the covenant of works reaches across the doctrine of man in the brief statement of faith which served the Presbyterian Church, U.S., from 1913 to 1962:

> He made man after his own image; male and female created he them, with immortal souls, endowed with knowledge, righteousness, and holiness, having the law of God in their hearts and power to fulfill it, and yet under a possibility of transgression, being left to the freedom of their own will.[1]

Imaging God, man was created and lives under an indelible law, while redemption is allied with grace, and, though well endowed, this natural and representative man is thereafter left to the autonomous liberty of his own will that he may fulfill his destiny in law. True enough that this man born under law may and ought to be born again into another, evangelical responsibility superposed on the first. But this regeneration gave him a double destiny, and the duty into which he was adopted never wholly erased that of his generation.

Nor in these years did this fail to make its way into the grass roots of the church. However neglected the Shorter Catechism may have been, few who now read these words and were reared Presbyterians were not at a formative age sufficiently exposed that its two most memorable answers might do their work. Or if not the Shorter Catechism, then its widely used introduction, the *Catechism for Young Children*,[2] makes the same claims more simply. Whatever else he forgot, the catechumen remembered the joy of the opening answer about the chief end of man, coupled with the shudder soon to follow when he was pricked with his sinful want of conformity unto or transgression of the law of God. It did not take much exposure to either catechism, perhaps mediated through a zealous Sunday School teacher, to leave the impression of a moralistic God who above all else expects and demands obedience to his law, of a God who is very gracious indeed to those whom he adopts, but who, if this adoption failed, could swiftly retaliate with damning law; and the shadow side of this portrait of God was difficult to dislodge. It can be replied, of course, that even by Calvin's account, in a pedagogical setting, this approach of grace through law has a certain psychological and educational necessity. If prohibited in the Confession, it is legitimate in the Catechism.

But neither the neophyte nor his tutors knew how, when the law had stung, to deepen the dignity of man and the heinousness of sin by making sin an utter disgrace.

Even yet, it is a deeply rooted persuasion that the Reformed churches have seen the responsibility of man under law more effectively than other communions and ought to guard this distinctive insight—in the minds of some, to preserve it denominationally; in the minds of others, to contribute it to the church catholic and ecumenical. A recent statement finds that one of the "particular accents" of the Reformed witness is the responsibility of man under law. In "The Witness of the Reformed Churches," a paper presented to the 1964 General Assembly of the Presbyterian Church, U.S., in conversations concerning union with the Reformed Church in America, this primacy of law is cherished in a revealing statement, redeemed only by the caution which links obedience and gratitude in the closing sentence.

> In a world which is confused as to manner of life and which has lost a compelling sense of responsibility, we affirm our faith that God's will for human life has been made known in His law. The validity of that law has in no way been abrogated by the Gospel. This law which is written into the structure of creation has been clearly revealed in the law of the Old Testament and supremely in the law of Christ. We affirm that the meaning of life is to be found when men, in thanksgiving for God's mercy and forgiveness, daily increase in obedience to His revealed will.

This paragraph would never have been written so except for the polar master principle which has possessed Reformed theology. There is much that is commendable in it. But we have to ask, in this witness of the Reformed churches to the world, just how much of the old universal legal contract remains implicitly in the linkage of man's "manner of life" and "compelling sense of responsibility" with a divine law "written into the structure of creation," reasserted in the Old Testament and again even in the law of Christ. What kind of validity does this law have that not even the later gospel can "abrogate" it? The very vocabulary echoes federal thought with its insistence that the legal covenant is not abrogated by the gospel. Such a witness will, needless to say, take moral revisions with dismay (and perhaps confessional ones as well), and be rule-oriented even after grace obtains. Will it not have too frequent recurrence to these unalterable legal absolutes, and will not its grace secretly be often a matter of recalling them? To the extent to which man is responsible under law, these norms having a certain permanence, universality, and pre-eminence over the gospel, we maintain that this witness is yet accented more by the Calvinists than by Calvin.

Compared with the theological battles fought over other issues surrounding the Genesis sagas, it may be said that the abandoning of the first covenant hardly occasioned discussion at all. The reason is not that the covenant was unimportant for theology. The reason is that the covenant as a technical construction could be dismissed and yet the principal ingredients retained by such a comparatively easy adjustment. It really did not need to be abandoned at all. Indeed, it is indestructible, perennial, natural. It only apparently fell into disuse; there rose from its ashes equivalent certainties regarding the primacy of law in the divine-human order which continued to accent Reformed theology. A reason sometimes given for the preservation of the Westminster standards in churches considering revision (whether as prime standards or in a treasury of confessions) is that, however archaic its expression, they retain in its clearest expression this witness in which Reformed theology has invested so heavily—the last, most mature, and richest of the great confessional standards of the Reformation.

It requires a deep shaking of the foundations on which the Westminster Confession has long reposed the government of God to reverse the historic order of law and grace. In the reconstruction, one is tempted to an intermediate step: to put grace side by side with law, and to let both operate concurrently and somewhat paradoxically. In large measure this has been the net characteristic impact of the coexistent covenants in tension, and it might fairly be said to be the tone of the 1964 statement above. But the reconstruction is not done, the Reformed church is not reformed, until grace is established firmly and unambiguously at the center of God, with law clearly its instrument and means.

And until the presuppositions of the Confession have been thoroughly repudiated and reversed, Reformed theology can subordinate law to grace only contrary to its legacy. So long as we start with law, so long as this is what is written immutably and non-negotiably into creation, it is always law into which grace must be fitted. If the warp of the Confession is grace, its woof is law, and since this is so, this revision cannot be done with confessional updating, modification, and repair. The dialectic of covenants, alas, is not peripheral to, but the master principle of, the "system of doctrine" to which most Presbyterian churches yet require their leadership to subscribe, and to say that it is not requires either ignorance or mental reservation. It is precisely the "system" that is offensive and needs most urgently to be jettisoned. If our observations have not gone astray, the doctrine of the covenants discolors the concept of God, his grace and his righteousness, his judgment and his law; the concept of creation; the concept of man, his duty, his sin, his responsibility; the concept of Christ, his person, his atonement, and his salvation. If that is not a systemic malady, nothing is!

Even when the Confession is retired from the front line of service and put in the gallery of creeds, its successor has to speak of the primacy of grace in God despite the presence of this nearest ancestor. Retirement cloaks rather than exposes its inadequacies. We thereby forgo repentance. The transition to a wholly non-federal creed can successfully be made, as evidenced in the Confession of 1967, and historically the inclusion of the Westminster Confession among the classics of Reformed faith is unexceptional. But veneration of its merits should also include, lest by forgetting the past we be condemned to repeat it, a remembrance of birthrights despised, of wilderness wanderings, of ancient landmarks removed, of backsliding from Mt. Zion to Mt. Sinai, of the days when the tablets of the law escaped from the ark of the covenant.

The Reformer is perhaps not an infallible guide, for in him the claims of grace may reach sterilizing proportions. His quenching of man's abilities may lead, if not rightly then by misunderstanding, to a denigration and negation of man. Man's correspondence in grace empties man of his own reality and makes of him but a puppet. From this there is little relief for the Calvinist, of course, who even with the general covenant soon strips man of all ability and whose grace when and where it does come is equally sterilizing. But others may wonder about this responsible man who is engaged so to grace; is this indeed not another form of slavery? Perhaps. There will be a wistful, if not adamant, longing after autonomous freedom and morality. But that land of individualism, by report of many who have passed through it additionally to Calvin, is not Eden but a wilderness. It is without destiny, a solitary place where the burden of responsibility in fact enslaves, and there responsible and individual works are evanescent. They have abiding worth, rather, only as they are known to be realizations in us, transient though life may be, of the presence of an eternal contemporary in whom all value and good is originated and gathered. For those who catch this vision, that all man's worth is penultimate does not mean that man is evacuated by a heteronomous God who takes all, but rather that man is given all and thereby elevated and incorporated into the grandeur of God.

Perhaps it is only now, as evidenced by recent and continuing confessional strugglings, that Reformed theology is prepared to reverse the federal order of law and grace and to return to Calvin's grace and law. With that return, the autonomous law-keeping man of the Westminster Confession can regain his birthright and become the grace-receiving man of the Reformer himself. If God insists on answerability to his law, as Calvin maintains not less than the Calvinists, man does not discover in such morality his fullest responsibility. We know ourselves as responsible men only when we encounter a God of love and become answerable to his grace. Responsibility is not an obligation, but an invitation; not a task, but a gift; not a command to work and to choose, but a call to love and be loved; not so much God's precept as his promise.

The danger that has beset Reformed thought throughout its venture into covenant theology is that in its use of covenant, nature, law, and grace, it makes of the Christian faith something which comes in where human powers fail. Religion becomes synonymous with redemption, and man needs God only for the mending of life's wrongness, to rescue him from his irresponsibility. The authentic Reformed witness makes place for this, but goes beyond. Religion belongs not to the weakness of life, but to its strength. Man must have faith not just because he is a sinner, but because he is human. Man's fundamental need for communion with a gracious God springs not merely from his error, but more basically from his dignity as a being formed for grace. Grace belongs before sin, not less than after. In grace God made and makes a responsible man.

Notes

CHAPTER I. The Westminster Confession and Covenant Theology

1. Wolfgang Musculus, *Loci Communes Theologiae Sacrae* (1560, 1564, and Basel, 1599).
2. Zacharias Ursinus, *Catechesis, Summa Theologiae,* in *Opera Theologica* (Heidelberg, 1612), question 36, p. 15; Johannes Cocceius, *Summa Doctrinae de Foedere et Testamento Dei* (1648 and 1654), II, 1 ff., and IV, 1 ff. (translations are my own); Francis Burmann, *Synopsis Theologiae* (Amsterdam, 1699); Herman Witsius, *De Oeconomia Foederum Dei cum hominibus* (1677), reprinted as *The Economy of the Covenants Between God and Man,* tr. William Crookshank (London, 1837).
3. Amandus Polanus, *Syntagma Theologiae Christianae* (Hanover, 1625); J. H. Heidegger, *Corpus Theologiae* (Zurich, 1700); and Francis Turretin (Turrettinus), *Institutio Theologiae elencticae* (Geneva, 1688). (Translations are my own.)
4. Robert Rollock, *Treatise on Effectual Calling,* in *Select Works* (Edinburgh, 1849), I, 25.
5. See Leonard J. Trinterud, "The Origins of Puritanism," in *Church History,* Vol. XX (March 1951), pp. 48 ff.
6. Edward Fisher, *The Marrow of Modern Divinity* (1645). That the work is Fisher's has been disputed. William Ames, *Medulla Theologica* (Amsterdam, 1623). (Translations are my own.) The durability of this work is evidenced by its recent publication as *The Marrow of Theology* (Philadelphia: Pilgrim Press, 1968). John Ball, *Treatise on the Covenant of Grace* (London, 1645).
7. Charles Hodge, *Systematic Theology* (New York, 1871), II, 117 ff. For a study of the rise of federal theology see Gottlob Schrenk, *Gottesreich und Bund im älteren Protestantismus* (Gütersloh, 1923). See also the article "Covenant Theology" by W. Adams Brown in the *Encyclopedia of Religion and Ethics,* ed. James Hastings.
8. For instance: "Our own Calvin it is true fails to recall such a covenant [of works] in his eloquence . . ."—Melchior Leydecker of Utrecht, quoted in Heinrich Heppe, *Reformed Dogmatics* (London: George Allen & Unwin, 1950), p. 333. The latter is an excellent source book for many of these writings not now easily obtained.
9. Westminster Confession, VII, 2. The Confession will afterward be cited simply by chapter and article.
10. Turretin, *op. cit.,* VIII, iii, 4.
11. See, for example, *ibid.,* VIII, iii, 7.

12. *Ibid.*, XII, iv, 7.
13. VII, 1.
14. Heppe, *op. cit.*, p. 246.
15. Johannes Braun (1628–1708), *Doctrina Foederum sive Systema Theologiae Didacticae et Elencticae* (Amsterdam, 1688), I, iii, 3, 11–12. Heppe, *op. cit.*, p. 247. Braun was professor at Groningen.
16. Rollock, *op. cit.*, I, 25.
17. John Macpherson, *The Westminster Confession of Faith,* in the *Handbooks for Bible Classes* series, ed. Marcus Dods and Alexander Whyte (Edinburgh, 1881), p. 66.
18. Turretin, *op. cit.*, VIII, iii, 5.
19. Heidegger, *op. cit.*, IX, 12.
20. Hodge, *op. cit.*, II, 118; cf. Westminster Larger Catechism, questions 20 and 30; Shorter Catechism, question 12.
21. XXI, 1–6. This was originally and is still in many versions chapter XIX. Larger Catechism, questions 22, 92–97; Shorter Catechism, question 16.
22. Witsius, *op. cit.*, I, ix, 2 and 23, my translation.
23. Braun, *op. cit.*, cited in Heppe, *op. cit.*, pp. 318 f.
24. Fisher, *op. cit.*, Part I, II, ii, 6.
25. VII, 3.
26. Hodge, *op. cit.*, II, 368 f.
27. Heppe, *op. cit.*, p. 316.

CHAPTER 2. Calvin and the Order of Grace

1. *Institutes,* I, ii, 1, C.R. 2.34 f.: I, iii, 3, C.R. 2.38; II, vi, 1, C.R. 2.247; Com. on Gen. 1—8, *passim,* C.R. 23.13 ff.; Com. on Rom. 1—2, C.R. 49.7 ff.; Ser. on Eph. 5:11–14, C.R. 51.695. Unless otherwise indicated, excerpts from Calvin's *Institutes* are reprinted from the translation by John Allen (Philadelphia: Presbyterian Board of Christian Education, 1936), and excerpts from Calvin's *Commentaries* are reprinted from the Calvin Translation Society editions (Edinburgh, 1844–1856; Grand Rapids, Mich.: Wm. B. Eerdmans Publishing Co., 1948–1956). Translations of Calvin's sermons are my own.
2. Com. on Gen. 2:9, C.R. 23.39.
3. Com. on Gen. 1:26, C.R. 23.27; *Institutes,* I, xiv, 22, C.R. 2.133 f.
4. Com. on Ps. 8:6, C.R. 31.94, my translation.
5. Com. on Gen. 3:22, C.R. 23.79. See also Com. on Ps. 104:29, C.R. 32.95 f.; Com. on Rom. 4:21, C.R. 49.85.
6. *Instruction in Faith (1537),* tr. Paul T. Fuhrmann (Philadelphia: The Westminster Press, 1949), sec. 4.
7. Ser. on Job 22:23–30, C.R. 34.328 f. See also Ser. on Deut. 22:9–11, C.R. 28.35 ff. We frequently will supply emphasis to selected words and phrases to underscore points at issue.
8. Ser. on Eph. 1:19–23, C.R. 51.344.
9. Com. on Gen. 3:19, C.R. 23.75, my translation. See also Com. on Gen. 8:21, C.R. 23.141; Ser. on Deut. 30:15–20, C.R. 28.568 f.
10. Ser. on Job 5:17–18, C.R. 33.255.
11. Com. on Gen. 9:6, C.R. 23.147.

Notes

12. Ser. on Gal. 3:3–5, C.R. 50.475 f.

13. Com. on Acts 14:17, C.R. 48.329, my translation. See also Com. on Gen. 3:17, C.R. 23.73.

14. Com. on Jer. 5:25, C.R. 37.636, italics mine.

15. Com. on 1 Cor. 1:21, C.R. 49.326.

16. *Instruction in Faith (1537)*, sec. 3.

17. *Ibid.*, italics mine.

18. *Institutes*, I, x, 2, C.R. 2.72 f., my translation.

19. Com. on John 11:40, C.R. 47.268, my translation.

20. Com. on Zech. 12:10, C.R. 44.335.

21. Ser. on Deut. 4:19–24, C.R. 26.162.

22. Ser. on Gal. 3:15–18, C.R. 50.530.

23. Ser. on Job 33:1–7, C.R. 35.41 ff.

24. Com. on Ezek. 16:15, C.R. 40.348, italics mine.

25. Ser. on 1 Tim. 2:3–5, C.R. 53.151–5, *passim*. See also Com. on Ezek. 18:23, C.R. 40.445 f.; Com. on 2 Peter 3:9, C.R. 55.475 f.

26. *Institutes*, I, xviii, 3, C.R. 2.170 f. See also *Institutes*, III, xxiv, 17, C.R. 2.727 f.; Ser. on Deut. 5:28–33, C.R. 26.408 ff.; Com. on Ps. 81:13 f., C.R. 31.765 f.; Com. on Isa. 10:7, C.R. 36.216; Com. on Lam. 3:37 f., C.R. 39.588 ff. Interestingly, the clearest passages in *Institutes*, sermons, and commentaries tend to be late.

27. *Reply of Calvin to the Syndics of Geneva in the case of Troillet*, Oct. 6, 1552, C.R. 14.379 f., my translation.

28. Com. on John 3:17, C.R. 47.66, my translation and italics. See also Com. on John 20:23, C.R. 47.442.

29. Com. on Ps. 40:11, C.R. 31.414.

30. Com. on Hos. 2:14, C.R. 42.243.

31. Com. on Hos. 6:4, C.R. 42.326, italics mine.

32. *Institutes*, II, v, 19, C.R. 2.247. See also II, i, 12, C.R. 2.195.

33. Argument to the Com. on Gen., C.R. 23.10, my translation.

34. Ser. on Isa. 53:1–4, C.R. 35.610.

35. *Institutes*, III, xxi, 1, C.R. 2.678. See also "legal covenant" in III, xvii, 15, C.R. 2.603.

36. Cocceius, *Summa de Foed.*, III, 63.

37. Heppe, *op. cit.*, p. 246.

38. Archibald Alexander Hodge, *A Commentary on the Confession of Faith* (Philadelphia, 1869), p. 170.

39. R. L. Dabney, *Systematic and Polemic Theology* (Richmond: Presbyterian Committee of Publication, 1927), p. 302.

40. George S. Hendry, *The Westminster Confession for Today* (Richmond: John Knox Press, 1960), pp. 88, 89.

41. Fisher, *op. cit.*, Part I, I, iv.

CHAPTER 3. Man: His Duty and His Sin

1. Com. on Gen. 2:9, C.R. 23.39, italics mine.

2. Geneva Catechism, 1541, question 7.

3. *Institutes*, II, viii, 16, C.R. 2.310.

4. *Ibid.*, I, ii, 1–2, C.R. 2.34 f.

5. Com. on Ps. 78:21, C.R. 31.729 f., and 78:7, C.R. 31.724, altering the C.T.S. translation.
6. Ser. on Deut. 6:13–15, C.R. 26.459.
7. *Institutes*, II, i, 4, C.R. 2.178.
8. Ser. on 1 Tim. 1:14–15, C.R. 53.86.
9. Com. on Gen. 2:16, C.R. 23.44 f. See also Com. on Gen. 2:9, C.R. 23.39.
10. *Institutes*, II, viii, 5, C.R. 2.270.
11. Com. on Gen. 2:16, C.R. 23.44 f.
12. Com. on Gen. 2:9, C.R. 23.39.
13. Com. on 1 Tim. 4:3, C.R. 52.296.
14. *Institutes*, II, i, 4, C.R. 2.178.
15. Com. on Gen. 2:9, C.R. 23.38.
16. *Instruction in Faith (1537)*, sec. 1. See also Com. on Matt. 22:37, C.R. 45.611.
17. *Ibid.*, sec. 2. See also *Institutes*, I, ii, 1, C.R. 2.34 f.
18. Ser. on Gen. 22:9–14, C.R. 23.774 f.
19. Ser. on Eph. 1:1–3, C.R. 51.252.
20. Com. on 2 Cor. 7:1, C.R. 50.83.
21. XXI, 1.
22. Turretin, *op. cit.*, XII, iv, 7 and 12; VIII, iii, 4.
23. Ames, *op. cit.*, I, xxiv, 19.
24. Charles Hodge, *op. cit.*, II, 364.
25. Larger Catechism, questions 91 and 93.
26. Witsius, *op. cit.*, I, iii, 25.
27. Braun, *op. cit.*, cited in Heppe, *op. cit.*, p. 319.
28. *Institutes*, II, i, 4, C.R. 2.178.
29. Com. on Gen. 3:6, C.R. 23.60, my translation.
30. Com. on Isa. 10:21, C.R. 36.226.
31. Com. on Isa. 57:13, C.R. 37.315. This is also a frequent theme in the Com. on John, cf. on 15:22, C.R. 47.351, and on 8:24, C.R. 47.197.
32. *Institutes*, II, i, 4, C.R. 2.178 f.
33. Com. on Gen. 3:12, C.R. 23.67, and 3:6, C.R. 23.59.
34. Com. on James 1:15, C.R. 55.390 f.
35. *Institutes*, III, iii, 10, C.R. 2.441, quoting Augustine. My translation. See also II, i, 8, C.R. 2.183; Com. on 2 Peter 1:4, C.R. 55.447.
36. Com. on 1 John 2:16, C.R. 55.319 f.
37. Com. on Rom. 7:7, C.R. 49.124, my translation. See also Ser. on Deut. 5:21, C.R. 26.371 ff., esp. 382; Com. on Eph. 4:17, C.R. 51.205.
38. Com. on Exod. 20:17, C.R. 24.719. See also *Responsio contra Pighium de Libero Arbitrio*, C.R. 9.362.
39. *Institutes*, II, ii, 10, C.R. 2.193 f.
40. Ser. on Job 3:2–10, C.R. 33.144.
41. Ser. on Deut. 28:46–50, C.R. 28.443 f.
42. Com. on 1 Cor. 6:11, C.R. 49.394. See also Argument to Com. on Rom., C.R. 49.1.
43. Shorter Catechism, question 14. See also Westminster Confession, VI, 6.
44. Fisher, *op. cit.*, Part I, I, ii–iii.
45. Benedict Pictet (1655–1724), *Theologia Christiana* (Geneva, 1696), IV, iii. Pictet was professor of theology at Geneva after Turretin, his uncle. His *Christian Theology*, a shorter reproduction of Turretin's *Institutes*,

was read for centuries, being reprinted by the Presbyterian Church in 1845 at Philadelphia, translated by Frederick Reyroux.
46. Polanus, *op. cit.,* VI, 3.
47. Turretin, *op. cit.,* IX, vi, 1 ff., esp. 9.
48. Witsius, *op. cit.,* I, viii, 1.
49. *Ibid.,* III, i, 21 f.
50. William Bucan (Bucanus), *Institutiones Theologicae* (Geneva, 1609), XVI, 31, cited in Heppe, *op. cit.,* p. 338. Bucan was professor of theology at Lausanne.
51. The verb *licet,* "to be permitted," has been translated by John Allen "to be lawful," and the noun *libido,* "lust," as "lawless desires," *Institutes,* II, i, 4, C.R. 2.178 f. Neither in context constitutes a direct reference to law. *Lex,* "law," does not occur in the chapter.
52. Com. on Gen. 2:9, C.R. 23.39.
53. Witsius, *op. cit.,* I, i, 15.

CHAPTER 4. Law in Covenant and Nature

1. *Institutes,* II, x, 1, C.R. 2.313.
2. *Ibid.,* II, vii, 12, C.R. 2.261.
3. *Ibid.,* II, viii, 4, C.R. 2.269 f.
4. *Ibid.,* III, xvii, 6, C.R. 2.594. See also *Instruction in Faith (1537),* sec. 10.
5. Ser. on Gal. 3:19–20, C.R. 50.538.
6. Com. on Ps. 19:11, C.R. 31.203. See also Com. on Luke 17:7, C.R. 45.413 f.
7. Ser. on Gal. 2:14–16, C.R. 50.409.
8. Com. on Rom. 3:20, C.R. 49.57; Ser. on Gal. 3:21–35, C.R. 50.545.
9. Com. on Heb. 4:12, C.R. 55.52.
10. Ser. on Gal. 3:1–3, C.R. 50.465 f.
11. Ser. on Gal. 2:17–18, C.R. 50.434. See also Com. on Gal. 2:19, C.R. 50.197 f.; Com. on John 16:8, C.R. 47.358 f.; Com. on 2 Cor. 3:7, C.R. 50.42.
12. Ser. on Gal. 3:19–20, C.R. 50.537.
13. Fisher, *op. cit.,* Part I, II, ii, 3. See also Westminster Larger Catechism, question 95.
14. XXI, 1–2.
15. Turretin, *op. cit.,* XIII, xii, 2. See also Witsius, *op. cit.,* IV, iv, 47 ff.; Polanus, cited in Fisher, *op. cit.,* Part I, II, ii, 3; Ames, *op. cit.,* I, xxxix, 4 ff.
16. Fisher, *op. cit.,* Part I, II, ii, 3.
17. Com. on Rom. 2:14 f., C.R. 49.37 f.
18. Ser. on 1 Tim. 5:4–5, C.R. 53.456.
19. Com. on Mark 10:21, C.R. 45.540.
20. *Institutes,* III, xiv, 3, C.R. 2.565.
21. Com. on Exod. 20:17, C.R. 24.719. See also Com. on Rom. 7:7, C.R. 49.123 f.
22. *Institutes,* II, ii, 24, C.R. 2.205.
23. Com. on Eph. 4:17, C.R. 51.205, altering the C.T.S. translation.
24. Com. on Ps. 86:2, C.R. 31.792, my translation.

25. Ser. on Eph. 1:3–4, C.R. 51.260. See also Ser. on Eph. 1:15–18, C.R. 51.312.
26. Com. on Rom. 2:3–5, *passim,* C.R. 49.30 ff.
27. Com. on Hab. 2:4, C.R. 43.531.
28. Fisher, *op. cit.,* Part I, II, ii, 6.
29. Turretin, *op. cit.,* XII, iv, 9.
30. *Institutes,* II, ii, 22, C.R. 2.203.

CHAPTER 5. The Righteousness of God

1. *Institutes,* I, x, 2, C.R. 2.73, italics mine.
2. Com. on Jer. 9:23 f., C.R. 38.52 f.
3. Com. on Ps. 11:4, C.R. 31.123 f. See also Com. on Rom. 3:6, C.R. 49.50.
4. Com. on Ps. 51:14, C.R. 31.521.
5. Com. on Ps. 71:15, C.R. 31.658.
6. Com. on Ps. 98:1, C.R. 32.48.
7. Com. on Ps. 103:17, C.R. 32.82.
8. Com. on Micah 7:9, C.R. 43.415 f., my translation.
9. *Institutes,* III, xiii, 1 f., C.R. 2.559 f., my translation.
10. Com. on Rom. 3:26, C.R. 49.63 f., my translation and italics.
11. *Institutes,* III, xi, 8, C.R. 2.539, altering Allen's translation.
12. Ser. on Job 34:26–29, C.R. 35.181. See also Com. on Jer. 1:16, C.R. 37.489 f.
13. *Institutes,* II, i, 9, C.R. 2.183.
14. Ser. on Job 21:22–34, C.R. 34.259.
15. Com. on Rom. 3:6, C.R. 49.50, my translation and italics.
16. Com. on 2 Thess. 1:5, C.R. 52.189, my translation.
17. Ser. on Job 8:1–6, C.R. 33.372.
18. *Instruction in Faith (1537),* secs. 8 and 10.
19. *Ibid.,* sec. 11. See also *Institutes,* II, vii, 8, C.R. 2.259.
20. Com. on James 2:13, C.R. 55.402 f.
21. Com. on John 9:39, C.R. 47.233; Com. on John 16:11, C.R. 47.360 f.; Com. on Isa. 11:4, C.R. 36.238.
22. W. G. T. Shedd, *Dogmatic Theology* (New York, 1888), Vol. II, p. 361, italics mine.
23. Turretin, *op. cit.,* VIII, iii, 4.
24. *Ibid.,* XII, iv, 6–8.
25. *Ibid.,* III, xix, 1–3.
26. *Ibid.*
27. III, 7.
28. XXXV, 1–2.
29. Westminster Larger Catechism, question 94.
30. Turretin, *op. cit.,* VIII, iii, 17.
31. *Ibid.,* XII, iv, 6.
32. Fisher, *op. cit.,* Part I, II, i.
33. VIII, 4–5. See also Larger Catechism, questions 39, 48, 52.
34. Fisher, *op. cit.,* Part I, II, i.
35. A. A. Hodge, *op. cit.,* p. 207.
36. XIII, 3; VIII, 5 and 8. See also Larger Catechism, questions 38 and 71.

Notes

CHAPTER 6. Responsible Man: His Accountability

1. *Institutes,* II, viii, 2, C.R. 2.267, italics mine.
2. Ser. on Gen. 22:9–14, C.R. 23.774 f. See also *Institutes,* II, viii, 14, C.R. 2.276.
3. Ser. on Job 35:8–11, C.R. 35.240. See also Ser. on Deut. 8:1–4, C.R. 26.584 ff.
4. *Institutes,* I, ii, 1 f., C.R. 2.34 ff., italics mine.
5. Turretin, *op. cit.,* VIII, iii, 4.
6. XXI (or XIX), 5, discounting its use in the present chapter X (or XXXV), added in this century.
7. Westminster Larger Catechism, question 95, italics mine.
8. Turretin, *op. cit.,* VIII, iv, 14, and XI, xxii, 18.
9. Witsius, *op. cit.,* I, i, 15.
10. Turretin, *op. cit.,* XI, xxxiii, 7.
11. Com. on Luke 17:7–9, C.R. 45.413 f., italics mine.
12. Ser. on Eph. 5:18–21, C.R. 51.727 ff., italics mine.
13. VII, 2, and XXXV (or XXXIII), 1.
14. Herman Bavinck (1854–1921), *Magnalia Dei* (1909), in English translation as *Our Reasonable Faith* (Grand Rapids, Mich.: Wm. B. Eerdmans Publishing Co., 1956), pp. 271 f.
15. Ames, *op. cit.,* I, xxiv, 19.
16. Turretin, *op. cit.,* VIII, iii, 4.
17. Ser. on Job 33:1–7, C.R. 35.48, italics mine.
18. Ser. on Eph. 1:4–6, C.R. 51.274, italics mine.
19. Ser. on Eph. 1:17–18, C.R. 51.329 f.
20. Com. on John 3:16, C.R. 47.64.
21. *Institutes,* II, iii, 11, C.R. 2.221.
22. Ser. on Deut. 6:10–13, C.R. 26.450 f., italics mine.
23. *Institutes,* II, v, 18, C.R. 2.245, altering Allen's translation.
24. *Ibid.,* I, xv, 8, C.R. 2.142, altering Allen's translation.
25. *Ibid.*
26. *Ibid.,* II, v, 18, C.R. 2.245.
27. Ser. on Eph. 1:13–15, C.R. 51.305. See also Ser. on Eph. 2:8–10, C.R. 51.380 f.; compare these with *Institutes,* I, xv, 8, C.R. 2.142.
28. Ser. on Deut. 24:14–18, C.R. 28.188.
29. XI, 2 f., and XXX, 1.
30. Witsius, *op. cit.,* I, ii, 13. See also I, viii, 26.
31. Turretin, *op. cit.,* VIII, iv, 14.
32. IV, 2.

CHAPTER 7. Irresponsible Man: His Culpability

1. Ser. on 1 Tim. 5:7–12, C.R. 53.472. See also Com. on Rom. 4:15, C.R. 49.78 f.
2. Com. on Jer. 10:7, C.R. 38.67.
3. Argument to Com. on Gen., C.R. 23.7 ff., altering the C.T.S. translation.
4. *Institutes,* I, x, 2, C.R. 2.73.
5. Com. on Acts 14:17, C.R. 48.327 f., my translation.

6. Com. on Acts 17:27, C.R. 48.415 f., my translation.
7. Ser. on Deut. 29:1-4, C.R. 28.489.
8. Com. on 1 Cor. 1:21, C.R. 49.326.
9. Ser. on Eph. 3:9-12, C.R. 51.459 ff.
10. *Institutes,* II, ii, 22, C.R. 2.203 f.
11. Com. on 1 Cor. 1:21, C.R. 49.326.
12. Ser. on Gal. 3:11-14, C.R. 50.498 f.
13. Ser. on Gal. 3:21-25, C.R. 50.546.
14. Ser. on 1 Tim. 5:7-12, C.R. 53.469.
15. Turretin, *op cit.,* XII, vi, 6 and 12-17, *passim;* XII, iv, 9 and 11.
16. I, 1. See also Larger Catechism, questions 2 and 60.

CHAPTER 8. Reformed Responsible Man

1. *A Brief Statement of Belief,* 1913, for years printed and bound with the Presbyterian Church, U.S., edition of the Westminster Confession.
2. *Catechism for Young Children,* based on the Shorter Catechism, prepared by Joseph P. Engels in 1840 and perennially reprinted.